the fundamentals of
typography

contents

1

2

3

Gavin Ambrose & Paul Harris

University
for the
Creative Arts

Ashley Road
Epsom
Surrey
KT18 5BE

Tel: 01372 202461
E-mail: gatewayepsom@uca.ac.uk

the fundamentals of
typography

ava | Academia
the environment of learning

An AVA Book
Published by AVA Publishing SA
Rue des Fontenailles 16
Case Postale
1000 Lausanne 6
Switzerland
Tel: +41 786 005 109
Email: enquiries@avabooks.ch

Distributed by Thames & Hudson (ex-North America)
181a High Holborn
London WC1V 7QX
United Kingdom
Tel: +44 20 7845 5000
Fax: +44 20 7845 5055
Email: sales@thameshudson.co.uk
www.thamesandhudson.com

Distributed in the USA and Canada by:
Watson-Guptill Publications
770 Broadway
New York, New York 10003
Fax: +1 646 654 5487
Email: info@watsonguptill.com
www.watsonguptill.com

English Language Support Office
56a Chapel Road
Worthing
West Sussex BN11 1DQ
AVA Publishing (UK) Ltd.
Tel: +44 1903 204 455
Email: enquiries@avabooks.co.uk

ISBN 2-940373-45-0 and 978-2-940373-45-1

10 9 8 7 6 5 4 3 2 1

Design by Gavin Ambrose
www.gavinambrose.co.uk

Production and separations by
AVA Book Production Pte. Ltd., Singapore
Tel: +65 6334 8173
Fax: +65 6259 9830
Email: production@avabooks.com.sg

4

5

&

introduction

Language is the dress of thought
Samuel Johnson

Typography surrounds us: it adorns the buildings and the streets through which we pass, it is a component part of the ever-expanding variety of media we consume – from magazines, to television and the internet – and we even increasingly sport it on our clothing in the form of branding and symbolic messages.

The typography that is a fundamental part of our lives today is the culmination of centuries of development, as the letters that comprise the written word evolved and crystalised into the alphabets that are in common usage. Technology has played a central role in this development, affecting and changing the way that the marks we recognise as characters are made and presented. Through the development of the printing industry, technology gave birth to the concept of typography, the many different presentations of the same character set.

While this book provides a deep insight into the essence of typographical development from the base of its historical roots, it goes much further, as by necessity it deals with language and communication, two concepts to which typography is inextricably linked. As the 18th-century English writer Samuel Johnson said, 'Language is the dress of thought'. That being the case, typography can be viewed as one of the swatches of fabric from which that dress is made.

It is hoped that this volume will serve as a valuable source of typographical information with which informed design choices can be made, to add depth and context to a work. This book is also intended to be a source of creative inspiration through the visual exploration of typefaces over the ages.

a	B	C	d	E	f
American Typewriter Light	Busorama	Century Gothic	De Vinne	Empire	Wittenberger Fraktur MT
g	h	i	j	k	⎧
Georgia	Humanist 777	Impact	Joanna	Kis	Linear Konstrukt
m	n	0	P	q	R
Modern No. 20	Novarese	Onyx	Peignot Light	Quorum Black	Rosewood
S	t	U	V	W	X
Stop	Trixie Cameo	Univers 45	VAG Rounded	Windsor	Xoxoxa

y	Z
Yorstat	Zapfino

There are thousands of fonts available and used throughout the world and they each have a story to tell. This simple A–Z presentation of some of the rich and diverse variety of typefaces demonstrates the many nuances, styles, historical and cultural references that typography includes.

how to get the most out of this book

This book aims to give readers a thorough grounding in the fundamentals of the wide-ranging field of typography, from best practice guidelines to creative experimentation.

The first chapter of this book is devoted to the development of language and the history of type, which continues to affect current thinking and designs. Significant developments are thoroughly examined, and then briefly summarised for convenient reference.

Types of serif

Serifs are a key characteristic for identifying a typeface due to the variety of ways in which they have been employed throughout the development of typography. Serifs enhance the readability of a piece of text by helping the eye to advance from one character to the next. Many serif styles reflect the zeitgeist of a particular time, with some more ornate or bolder, while others are more discreet and refined. Some of the main serif styles are illustrated here.

Horizontal movement across the page…

This block is set in Apollo. The decorative serifs aid navigation by creating horizontal movement that leads the eye to track across the page. Below is Geometric 231.

in contrast to vertical solidity

Pictured right are the main serif varieties that are commonly found on serif form. Each type of serif lends a font its own personality, typographic traits and design impact - from the robust, muscular quality of an unbracketed slab serif, to the delicate fineness of a hairline serif. Although at times barely noticeable, typographical details such as serifs can alter how a piece of work is perceived. For this reason it is important for designers to bear them in mind and even celebrate the subtle differences they can give a job.

Unbracketed slab serif
A serif without any supporting brackets on ts-heavy slabs.

Bracketed slab serif
The slab serifs are supported by subtle curved brackets.

Bracketed serif
A serif with barely noticeable supporting brackets.

W

This is Egizians Classic Antique Black which has large slab serifs with no supporting brackets.

Clarendon is also a slab serif but it has small arcs that bracket the serifs.

Berkeley also has small bracken on its serifs, which are of a regular size.

Left
This book by Studio EA uses an overly large and exaggerated bracketed serif font to create a typographic execution reminiscent of the 1970s.

Left
The dairy signage uses a font with tapering slur serifs.

Above
The stamp features exaggerated wedge serifs.

Unbracketed serif
A standard serif without brackets.

Hairline serif
A fine hairline serif without brackets.

Wedge serif
The serif is shaped like a wedge rather than the typical rectangle or line shape.

Slur serif
Rounded serifs that look 'unfocused'.

W

Memphis has regular-sized serifs without brackets.

Printer Bodoni has thin hairline serifs that give it a more refined air.

The brackets on the serifs of Egyptian 505 are exaggerated into more noticeable wedges.

Cooper Black has rounded, bobbly serifs that go with its unique visual form and give the impression that it is out of focus.

Each subsequent chapter focuses on one aspect of typography such as the basics or using type. The book is logical and progressive, with each chapter providing an information base for the next. Explanatory text is illustrated with numerous examples of typefaces and the use of type in context, with some analytical commentary. Key concepts are explained in detail, in pullout boxes and worked examples.

The font index and general index at the back of the book enable the book to be used as an easy reference guide.

Relative and absolute measurements

Typography uses two types of measurements, *absolute measurements* and *relative measurements*. It is important to understand the differences between these to understand many of the typographic processes.

Absolute measurements

Absolute measurements are easy to understand as they are measurements of fixed values. For example, a millimetre is a precisely defined increment of a centimetre. Equally, points and picas, the basic typographic measurements, have fixed values. All absolute measurements are expressed in finite terms that cannot be altered. Pictured below are four measurement systems that express the same physical distance.

Relative measurements

In typography, many measurements, such as character spacing, are linked to type size, which means that their relationships are defined by a series of relative measurements. Ems and ens for example are relative measurements that have no prescribed, absolute size. Their size is relative to the size of type that is being set.

Leading is another example of the use of relative measurement. Most desktop publishing programs assign an automatic percentage value for functions like leading. The characters below (far left) are 10pt, so with leading set at 120 percent, they are effectively being set on 12pt leading. As the type gets bigger, so does the leading as it is relative to the type size.

If this did not happen and the leading remained constant, as the characters get bigger they would eventually crash into one another, as in the bottom row.

Points

The point is the unit of measurement used to measure the type size of a font, for example, 7pt Times New Roman. This measurement refers to the height of the type block, not the letter itself as shown below (right). This basic typographical measurement is an absolute measurement equivalent to 1/72 of an inch or 0.35mm and its creation is attributed to French clergyman Sébastien Truchet (1657-1729). It was further developed by Pierre Fournier and Francois Didot in the 19th century, before the British/American or Anglo Saxon point was defined as 1/72 of an inch.

Type sizes traditionally bore a relationship to the 72 point inch (six picas) but with digitised PostScript typefaces, it is now easy to use irregular sizes such as 10.2pt. This relationship is reflected in the old naming system for these common sizes, with 12pt type being referred to as *Pica*. Some of the other names have a looser connection, and indeed the sizes are only approximate translations to the modern point equivalents. These names are no longer in common use, but the equivalent sizes are, with most software packages using these as the default sizes.

	Minion	Bourgeois	Long Primer	Pica	English	Great Primer	2-line Pica	2-line Great Primer	Canon or 4-line
Before standardisation, typefaces of similar names had varying sizes. A Pica from one type foundry would be exactly 12 points, while the same measurement from another could vary by as much as a point.	7	9	10	12	14	18	24	36	48

Brj Brj

As the point size of a typeface refers to the height of the type block and not the letter itself, different typefaces of the same size behave differently, as these two examples above set in 72pt type show. While they are the same size the characters do not necessarily extend to the top or bottom of the block, which has an impact on leading values discussed on *page 124*. The typefaces shown above are Futura (left), and Foundry Sans (right).

Picas

A pica is a unit of measurement equal to 12 points that is commonly used for measuring lines of type. There are six picas (or 72 points) in an inch, which is equal to 25.4 millimetres. This is the same for both a traditional pica and a modern PostScript pica. There are six PostScript picas to an inch.

The measurement of a piece of movable type is entire vertical size, not just a measure of the character height.

| 3 inches (3") |
| 76.2 millimetres (76.2mm) |
| 216 points (216pt) |
| 18 picas (18 pica) |

1"   6 Picas

1

Type has developed over the last 600 years as the printing process has evolved. The characters that are printed, however, have been developed over a much longer time period as language itself has developed from Egyptian hieroglyphs to the Latin letters we use today.

a brief history

Thomas Theodor Heine's illustration created for the cover of the German satirical magazine *Simplicissimus* that he co-founded in 1895.

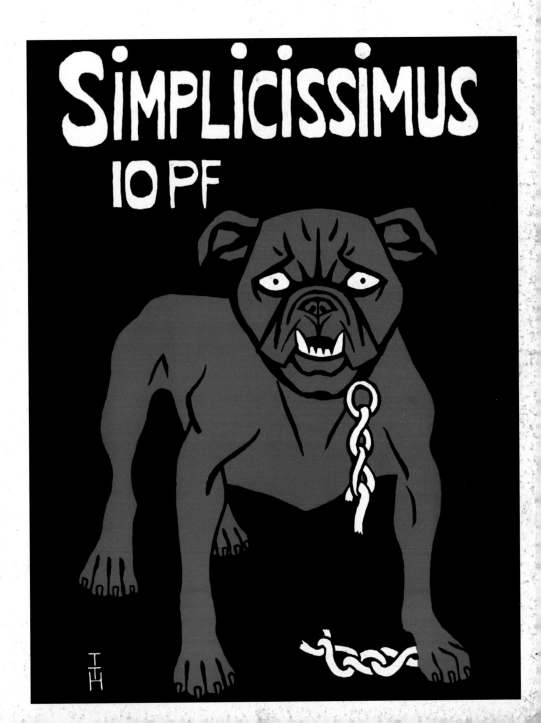

The history of type

Type is the means by which an idea is written and given visual form. Many typefaces in use today are based upon designs created in earlier historical epochs, and the characters themselves have a lineage that extends back thousands of years to the first mark-making by primitive man, when characters were devised to represent objects or concepts.

This section is an introduction to the complex origins of type. An appreciation of typography naturally involves understanding how written language developed. While a general timeline is presented here, many elements and the technological advances that made developments possible overlap between epochs. For instance, moveable type is generally credited to Johannes Gutenberg, a German goldsmith and printer, in the 1440s. Counter claims to the invention include Laurens Janszoon Coster in the Netherlands and Panfilo Castaldi in Italy. The true origins of this lay much earlier though, with the forerunner of Gutenberg's revolutionary system being invented by Bi Sheng in China between 1041 and 1048. Further refinements were made during the Goryeo Dynasty of Korea by Chwe Yun-Ui in about 1234, where metal was first used instead of brittle clay or easily damaged wood.

As type mechanics, and typography as an art, developed simultaneously in several pockets of the world it can be hard to be definite. This section aims to be as comprehensive as possible, but it is impossible to be conclusive. One of the wonders of typography is this fluidity, its ability to adapt to circumstances, technological advances and cultural shifts.

Type's key role in communication means that it can often be tied to a specific event in history or cultural epoch. Pictured (left to right): an early German Bible; the US Declaration of Independence signed 4th July 1776; a postage stamp from the Nazi regime; and the Vietnam War Wall Memorial, Washington D.C.

Type occupies a formal role in the recording of history. The permanence of the carved word and the value of the printed item are inseparable from our cultural heritage as type helps us to record, celebrate and remember.

Language is not static

Letters, language and indeed typography develop and change over time as the dominant power inherits, alters, adapts and imposes its will on existing forms. The modern Latin alphabet is a result of this ongoing transition that has been performed over several millennia. For example, the modern letter 'A' was originally a pictogram representing an ox's head, but as the Phoenicians wrote from right to left, the symbol was turned on its side. Under the Greek civilisation this character was turned again as the Greeks generally (though not always, *see page 20*), wrote from left to right. Finally, the Romans turned the character full-circle, giving it the form that we recognise today.

A pictogram of an ox's head…

…has been turned on its side by the Phoenicians…

Rotated by the Greeks…

…and turned upright by the Romans, to form the modern 'A'.

Latin

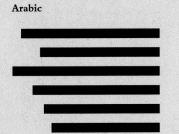

Arabic

Chinese

Boustrophedon

Reading direction

The direction in which text is read varies and is based on historical factors such as how text used to be written. For example, Chinese calligraphers use a paint brush to draw ideograms and so it is easier to write down the page. Carving stone tablets by moving from right to left allows you to read what you have written, while the natural motion for writing with a pen (for right-handed people) is moving from left to right. Pictured are outlines for four systems: Latin, Arabic, Chinese and the Greek boustrophedon system.

Cuneiform tablets

Cuneiform uses a wedge-shaped stylus to make impressions into a wet clay tablet and is the earliest standardised writing system, which was developed in ancient Mesopotamia, the region that is now east of the Mediterranean, from about 4,000 BC until about 100 BC.

Early forms of cuneiform were written in columns from top to bottom, but later changed to be written in rows from left to right. With this change the cuneiform signs were turned on their sides.

Cuneiform began to die out as other language systems such as Aramaic spread through the region in the 7th and 6th centuries BC, and as the use of Phoenician script increased.

Above
Cuneiform, the earliest known form of writing, on a clay tablet.

Right
Cuneiform tablet detail.

Far right
Mesopotamia, modern Syria, is where cuneiform originated.

Some terms to be familiar with
There are many terms used within this book that you'll need to be familiar with, many of which are often confused.

PHONOGRAM
A written symbol, letter, character or other mark that represents a sound, syllable, morpheme or word.

IDEOGRAM
A graphic element that represents an idea or a concept.

ICON
A graphic element that represents an object, person or something else.

SYMBOL
A graphic element that communicates the ideas and concepts that it represents rather than denoting what it actually is.

PICTOGRAM
A graphic element that describes an action or series of actions through visual references or clues.

Hieroglyphs

Hieroglyphs are a pictogrammatic writing system developed by several cultures including the ancient Egyptians and Incas. Each pictogram represents an object such as an animal, tool or person rather than vocal sounds. In Egypt, they were developed by scribes to record the possessions of the Pharaoh, by drawing a picture of a cow or a boat for example. As more complex ideas needed to be recorded, written language became more complex as more pictograms were needed. Eventually there were over 750 individual Egyptian pictograms.

Hieroglyphs can be written from right to left, left to right, or downwards, which can be discerned by seeing which way pictures of people or animals face. The text is read towards the faces. For example, if they are facing to the left, the inscription is read from left to right.

Right
Hieroglyphs on papyrus, reading downwards, indicated by the border lines.

Top left
Depiction of the god Anubis at Queen Hatshepsut's temple, Egypt.

Bottom left
Hieroglyphs and ceiling painting in Hatshepsut's temple, Deir el-Bahari (Thebes), Egypt.

Left
Hieroglyphs on obelisk.

The important developments in summary:
The allocation of meaning to symbols

Codification of specific meanings to particular symbols

Visual representation of complex ideas

Structure for writing and reading symbols

Ideogram-based languages

Ideogrammatic languages use characters or symbols to represent an idea or concept without expressing the pronunciation of a particular word or words. Ideogrammatic languages have a one-to-one relation between a symbol and an idea that functions in a similar way to the red road sign with a horizontal white bar that means 'no entry'. The meaning is understood but there is no indication of how this is vocalised. Ideogrammatic languages, traditionally written down the page, include Chinese, Japanese, Korean and Thai.

The important developments in summary:
Separation of sign and signified

Coupling of ideograms to form words

Using words to express abstract concepts

Above
These Chinese ideograms represent the four seasons (left to right) spring, summer, autumn and winter.

Above
These Chinese ideograms represent (left to right) sake, beautiful and sushi.

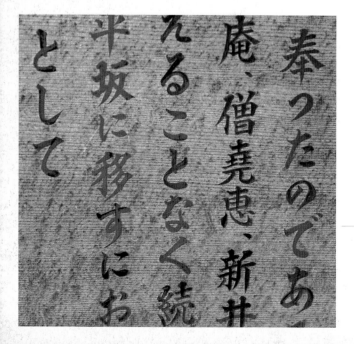

Far left
Hiragana and Kanji Japanese characters.

Left
Korean words for (top to bottom) peace, angel, spirit, charm and beauty – all made with ideograms.

Right
The Japanese Katakana alphabet.

Far right
Stamp from China.

Chinese and Japanese scripts

Written Chinese assigns a single distinctive symbol, or character, to each word. Many symbols have remained fundamentally the same for over 3,000 years even though the writing system has been standardised and stylistically altered. The system became word-based to express abstract concepts, with ideograms representing sounds rather than concepts. Shi Huangdi, the first emperor of unified China, enforced a standardised writing called small seal. This developed into regular and running scripts in the Han dynasty (206 BC–AD 220). Printed Chinese is modelled on the standard script.

Japanese writing began in the 4th century, using imported Chinese script. A system emerged in which Chinese characters were used to write Chinese words and their Japanese equivalents, and were also used for their phonetic values to write grammatical elements. These were simplified and eventually became the syllabic scripts (an alphabet consisting of symbols for consonants and vowels) Hiragana and Katakana.

Modern Japanese is written with these two scripts and/or up to 10,000 Chinese Han or Kanji characters. Texts may also include Romaji, the standard way of transliterating Japanese into the Latin alphabet. The Japanese use Romaji characters on computers that are converted to Kanji, Hiragana or Katakana characters by software.

私　　わたし　ワタシ　Watashi　　　I

Kanji　　　　　**Hiragana**　　　　　**Katakana**　　　**Romaji**　　　**English**

アカサタナハマヤラワ
イキシチニヒミリウン
エケトノスツヌフムユ
ルレセテネヘメオコソ
ホモヨロヲン

Phoenician characters

The Phoenicians lived in the eastern Mediterranean in what is modern day Lebanon. They developed the basis of the modern Latin alphabet around 1600 BC and formalised a system of 22 'magic signs' or symbols that represented sounds rather than objects. The symbols could be put together in different combinations to construct thousands of words, even though the alphabet only contained consonants and had no vowels. Phoenician was written horizontally from right to left without spaces between words, although dots were sometimes used to denote word breaks. The Phoenician alphabet is the bedrock for many subsequent writing systems including Arabic, Hebrew, Greek and Latin, and ultimately for the modern European alphabet that is used today.

The important developments in summary:
22 symbols representing sounds not objects

Coupling of sounds to form words

Precursor of subsequent writing systems

Emergence of main characters of the modern Western alphabet

Some terms to be familiar with
Linguistics – the science of language – uses the following terms to describe various elements of language and speech.

Phoneme
A phoneme describes a speech sound or sign element – the basic unit that distinguishes between different words. For example, the phonemes 'o' and 'x' come together to make 'ox'.

D I S C R E D I T E D

Morpheme
A morpheme is a distinctive group of phonemes that form the smallest language unit that has a semantic interpretation. A word can be broken into a series of morphemes, with each having a distinct meaning. The word 'discredited' has three morphemes; 'dis', 'credit' and 'ed'.

DIS CREDIT ED

Syllable
A syllable is a unit of spoken language consisting of a single, uninterrupted sound. This may be formed by a vowel, diphthong, a syllabic consonant alone, or by any of these sounds accompanied by one or more consonants. The word 'discredited' has four syllables.

DIS CRED IT ED

Letter
A letter is a mark or glyph (symbol) used in an alphabetic writing system to indicate a sound.

D I S C R E D I T E D

The 22 magic signs

The Phoenicians were responsible for what is arguably the development of the greatest invention of humanity. The alphabet of 22 magic signs (below) that they are believed to have developed at Byblos and left to the world were the basis of subsequent languages such as Greek, Hebrew and Latin.

The 22 signs are pictured below along with their Latin equivalents and the objects that they are believed to have originally represented. Many characters such as 'O', 'W', 'K' and 'X' are perfectly recognisable and have changed little through the centuries.

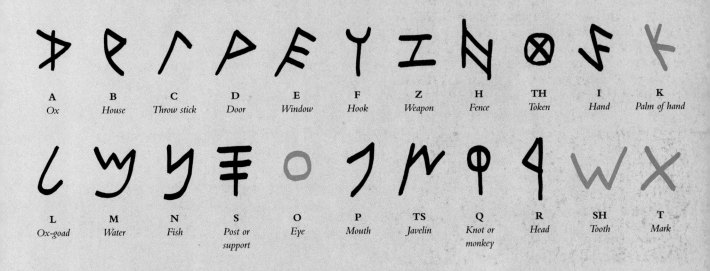

A	B	C	D	E	F	Z	H	TH	I	K
Ox	*House*	*Throw stick*	*Door*	*Window*	*Hook*	*Weapon*	*Fence*	*Token*	*Hand*	*Palm of hand*

L	M	N	S	O	P	TS	Q	R	SH	T
Ox-goad	*Water*	*Fish*	*Post or support*	*Eye*	*Mouth*	*Javelin*	*Knot or monkey*	*Head*	*Tooth*	*Mark*

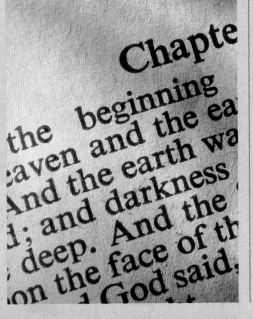

Byblos

Byblos (modern day Jubayl in Lebanon) was a Phoenician Mediterranean seaport that exported papyrus, and from which the word Bible is derived. It is thought that the residents of this city reduced the number of symbols in the Phoenician alphabet to the 22 pictured above.

Far left
Modern day Beirut, Lebanon, 2001.

Left
A detail from the Bible.

The Greek alphabet

The Greeks adopted the characters of the Phoenician system, such as aleph (a) and beth (b), from which they developed their alphabet. Indeed, the word alphabet is the union of the Greek characters alpha and beta (right). By around 800 BC the Greeks had added other characters to their alphabet, which became the basis of the modern day Hebrew and Arabic scripts. Early Greek was written in the boustrophedon style (*see opposite page*) where rather than proceeding from left to right as in modern English, or right to left as in Arabic, alternate lines must be read in opposite directions. Many ancient Mediterranean languages were typically written in this style. The development of punctuation allowed writing to move away from the boustrophedon style towards a system that reads left to right. As this happened, many symbols were rotated to make them easier to write.

Many Greek letters have a legacy in everyday speech such as 'alpha male' and 'beta testing', as their symbols are used

as mathematical symbols i.e. pi (π). Writing became more standardised around 500 BC when the character set became fully recognisable as that which we know today in both the Greek and Roman forms.

Aleph Beth
Alpha Beta
AlphaBeta
Alphabet

Above
The transition of Phoenician characters into Greek, and ultimately, into words we recognise today.

The important developments in summary:
Introduction of spaces and vowels

A move away from the boustrophedon system of writing

Above
A Greek inscription on the Xanthian obelisk in the ruined Lycian city of Xanthos, Turkey. The text is presented without letterspacing and without the use of punctuation.

α	Alpha		ο	Omicron
β	Beta		π	Pi
γ	Gamma		ρ	Rho
δ	Delta		σ	Sigma
ε	Epsilon		τ	Tau
ζ	Zeta		υ	Upsilon
η	Eta		φ	Phi
θ	Theta		χ	Chi
ι	Iota		ψ	Psi
κ	Kappa		ω	Omega
λ	Lambda			
μ	Mu			
ν	Nu			
ξ	Xi or Si			

Above
The 24 characters from the modern Greek alphabet and their Greek names.

Boustrophedon writing

The boustrophedon writing style is called the 'ox plough method' because the lines of text are written and read in opposite directions. The text moves across the page from left to right, drops down a line and then comes back from right to left and so on down the page as shown in the diagram. This is not as simple as it may seem as there are three methods of doing this: the lines reverse, the lines and words reverse, or the lines, words and letters all reverse.

A modern example of boustrophedon writing is the word 'Ambulance' that is written backwards on the bonnet of an ambulance so that it can be read correctly when seen in the rear-view mirror of cars in front of it.

Above
A block of marble inscribed with Greek text.

Vowels and spaces

The Greeks developed vowels, which created a complete and flexible phonetic alphabet. The insertion of spaces between words and diacritical marks *(see page 92)* was a further development that helped facilitate reading and comprehension.

A E I O U
CNYRDTHS
CAN YOU READ THIS

Above
The use of vowels and spaces makes text easier to read and understand.

Cyrillic languages

Cyrillic alphabets are those based on Glagolitic (an alphabet developed by missionaries during the 9th century to translate the Bible for the Great Moravia region) and used for Slavic languages such as Russian. They are named after Byzantine missionary St Cyril and developed from Greek between the 8th and 10th centuries, possibly by St Kliment of Ohrid for the Old Church Slavonic language. The current Cyrillic alphabet was adopted in 1708 during the reign of Peter the Great of Russia, with a further modification in 1917/18 when four letters were eliminated. The Cyrillic alphabet is the basis of over 50 different languages in Russia, Central Asia and Eastern Europe, many of which use additional characters that have been adapted from standard Cyrillic letters, with others taken from the Greek or Latin alphabets.

Cyrillic languages include: Abaza, Abkhaz, Adyghe, Avar, Azeri, Balkar, Belarusian, Bulgarian, Chechen, Chukchi, Church Slavonic, Chuvash, Dungan, Evenk, Gagauz, Ingush, Kabardian, Kazakh, Komi, Kurdish, Kyrghyz, Lezgi, Lingua Franca Nova, Macedonian, Moldovan, Mongolian, Old Church Slavonic, Russian, Ruthenian, Serbian, Slovio, Tajik, Tatar, Turkmen, Ukrainian, Uighur, Uzbek, Yakut and Yupik.

Above
The Russian MIR orbital station. The reversed 'N' denotes the letter 'I', and a 'P' sounds as 'R'.

Right
Detail from a Russian dictionary, demonstrating that some Cyrillic characters are adapted from other alphabetical systems. This 'borrowing' occurs with several characters such as the Greek Phi symbol Pi (P) that reappears as the Cyrillic character 'P', an upturned Latin 'V', an inverted 'R' and a numeral '3'.

Below left
A Russian stamp showing Cyrillic characters.

The Cyrillic alphabet

The Cyrillic alphabet has 33 letters, including 21 consonants and ten vowels, and two letters without sounds that represent hard and soft signs. It is used to write six natural Slavic languages (Belarusian, Bulgarian, Macedonian, Russian, Serbian and Ukrainian) in addition to many other languages of the former Soviet Union, Asia and Eastern Europe.

Late medieval Cyrillic letters tended to be very tall and narrow, with strokes often shared between adjacent letters. Peter the Great mandated the use of westernised letterforms, which have been adopted in the other languages that use the alphabet. This means that modern Cyrillic fonts are very similar to modern Latin fonts of the same font families. Lowercase Cyrillic letterforms are essentially smaller versions of the capitals, apart from the 'a', 'e' and 'y' that are Western shapes, rather than straightforward reductions of capital letterforms.

R Я V Λ

The Russian alphabet

The 33 Russian Cyrillic lowercase and uppercase letters are shown in magenta, with their English transliteration in black. Russian punctuation follows similar conventions to German, such as the use of commas to offset subordinate and coordinate clauses, and spacing of letters in different ways to show emphasis.

а	А	a	и	И	i	с	С	s	ъ	Ъ	"
б	Б	b	й	Й	j	т	Т	u	ы	Ы	y
в	В	v	к	К	k	у	У	u	ь	Ь	'
г	Г	g	л	Л	l	ф	Ф	f	э	Э	eh
д	Д	d	м	М	m	х	Х	kh	ю	Ю	yu
е	Е	e	н	Н	n	ц	Ц	ts	я	Я	ya
ё	Ё	ee	о	О	o	ч	Ч	ch			
ж	Ж	zh	п	П	p	ш	Ш	sh			
з	З	z	р	Р	r	щ	Щ	shch			

Semitic and Aramaic languages

Aramaic developed from Phoenician around 900 BC in what is modern Syria and south east Turkey. It is a Semitic language that was a precursor for Arabic and Hebrew, which it closely resembles. Aramaic was used and spread by the Assyrian empire and the Babylonian and Persian empires that followed it, taking the language as far as India and Ethiopia. Towards the end of the 6th century BC, the early Aramaic alphabet was replaced by the Hebrew square script, which is also (confusingly) known as the Aramaic alphabet. As Aramaic was the language of empire, many parts of the Old Testament were originally written in this language, as were the Dead Sea Scrolls. Aramaic is still spoken in parts of Syria, Iraq, Turkey and Iran.

Aramaic letterforms
The 22 characters of the Aramaic alphabet and their Latin equivalents.

Arabic

Modern day Arabic, like Phoenician, is written and read right to left. Arabic is based on the 22 consonants of the Phoenician alphabet with an optional marking of vowels using diacritics. Arabic script uses the Aramaic letter names (Alef, Jeem, Dal, Zai, Sheen, and so on). This alphabet contains 18 letter shapes but by adding one, two, or three diacritical marks to letters that serve as vowel sounds a total of 28 letters is obtained, as illustrated below. These diacritical marks originate in Hebrew and Aramaic and were added so that Muslims of non-Arab origin could correctly pronounce the Koran, their holy text.

ا	ب	ت	ث	ج	ح	خ	ر	ذ	د	ز	س	ش	ص	ض
a	b	t	th	j	ḥ	kh	d	dh	r	z	s	sh	ṣ	ḍ

ط	ظ	ع	غ	ف	ق	ك	ل	م	ن	ه	و	ي
ṭ	z	c	gh	f	q	k	l	m	n	h	w	y

Arabic letterforms
The 28 characters of the Aramaic alphabet and their Latin equivalents.

Hebrew

Hebrew is a Semitic language. Its alphabet is adapted from Aramaic and evolved into a script called Square Hebrew, which is the source of modern Hebrew printing. The Hebrew alphabet has 22 letters, all consonants, with vowel symbols placed below the consonants if required.

Left
A page from the Koran, 1780–1800 showing text reading right to left.

Above
The letters of the Hebrew alphabet (top); their use on a monument (middle); and in a page from the Torah, the Jewish religious book.

Above
Arabic characters form part of the decoration of this building.

Above
A page of modern Hebrew text, reading right to left.

The Roman alphabet

The 26-letter Roman alphabet that we use today was formed from the Greek alphabet and spread through the Roman empire. Majuscules or uppercase letters derive directly from the forms carved in stone by the Romans, which serve as the basis for many modern day typefaces, and from where we get the name Roman. Roman is now used to describe the basic letterforms, principally the minuscules (lowercase letters), even though the name is derived from the majuscule forms.

Times New Roman, Stanley Morison / Victor Lardent, 1932
Commissioned by *The Times* of London after Morison criticised the newspaper for being badly printed and typographically behind the times. Based on Plantin, but revised for legibility and economy of space, it was called Times New Roman to counterpoint the 'Times Old Roman' the newspaper previously used.

TIMES NEW ROMAN

Above
Detail from the Roman Stadium, Pompeii, Italy. The angular carvings that have inspired many subsequent typefaces are given extra dimension over time as dirt build-up in the recesses creates visual depth.

Trajan, Carol Twombly, 1989
Modern typefaces such as Trajan (below) have their roots in stone carving from the Roman era. Typographer Twombly was influenced by early Roman forms in this design, which is modern yet steeped in historical reference.

ABCDEFGHIJKLMNOPQRSTUVWXYZ 1234567890

Numerals

The Romans used seven of their letterforms as base numerals, with each letter representing a numeric building block as pictured (below). Numbers are constructed by stringing the blocks together. For example 2006 is MMVI. With this system the Romans did not need a character for '0'.

The important developments in summary:
Development of 26-letter Roman alphabet

Appearance of stone-carved majuscules

Letter-based number system

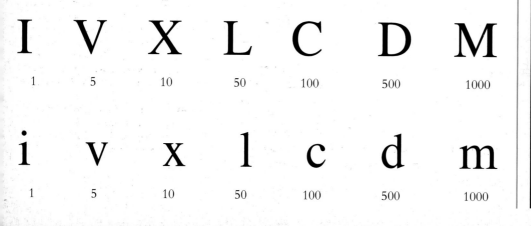

I	V	X	L	C	D	M
1	5	10	50	100	500	1000

i	v	x	l	c	d	m
1	5	10	50	100	500	1000

ET &   & & &
⦿   Et &

The ampersand

The ampersand character is a ligature of the letters of the Latin word *et*, which means 'and'. The name 'ampersand' is a contraction of the phrase 'and per se and', which translates as 'the symbol for and by itself means and'. The earliest usage of the symbol dates back to the 1st century AD and it is now found in many languages that use the Latin alphabet.

The provenance of the ampersand can be clearly seen in some typefaces. Several examples of the ampersand can be seen above. The 'E' and 'T' can easily be distinguished in Caslon Antique (top left) and in its italic 540 counterpart (top centre). The Roman version (top right), however, is more abstract, as is Univers black (bottom right). Rotis Sans Serif (centre bottom) provides a modern twist that once again separates the letters, while Robotnik (bottom left) uses an abstract symbol instead of following any convention.

CAROLINE MINUSCULE, ALCUIN OF YORK AND THE EFFECT OF THE RENAISSANCE

Charlemagne, or Charles the Great, regarded as the founder of the Holy Roman empire, began to standardise all ecclesiastical texts around 800. Alcuin of York, Abbot of Saint Martin of Tours, and his workforce of monks endeavoured to rewrite all religious texts. For this they devised a print system including *majuscules*, or uppercase letterforms, and *minuscules*, or lowercase forms. These became known as the Caroline minuscules and would later become the basis of modern typography.

With the demise of the Charlemagne rule, regional variations on this theme appeared. Blackletter became popular in Northern Europe and remained in widespread use for over 400 years. Later, in Italy, scholars of the Renaissance period were rediscovered classic Roman and Greek works. They mistook the Caroline form as being much older, not initially realising that these books had been rewritten between 796-804. Adapting their rotunda script (a broad open character), a hybrid humanistic script was born – the *scrittura humanistica*. Modern descendants of this form are evident today – Optima, shown on page 43, clearly has its roots in the calligraphic style.

The Renaissance, or rebirth, began in Italy in the 14th century with the revival of interest in classical art and the classical world of ancient Greece, as people sought to move away from the dogma of religion that dominated the Middle Ages.

Pictured above is *Venus of Urbino* painted by Titian in 1538, that is exhibited in the Uffizi Gallery in Florence, Italy.

The modern alphabet

The modern Latin alphabet consists of 52 upper- and lowercase letters with ten numerals and a variety of other symbols, punctuation marks and accents that are employed by various different languages. Lowercase letters developed from cursive (joined up) versions of the uppercase letters.

ABCDEFGHIJKLMNOPQRSTUVWXYZabcdefghij
klmnopqrstuvwxyz1234567890§-=[];'\`,./±!@£$
%^&*()_+{}:"|~<>?¡#¢¶•—≠Œ®†¥Ø"Åß ƒ©·°
…Æ«Çµ÷ÅÄÊÎÔÛÙØUÁÉÍÓÚåäêîôûøuáéíóú

Perpetua, Eric Gill, 1928
The characters above set in Perpetua are the full set for the English alphabet. Formal looking Perpetua is based on designs from old engravings and has small, diagonal serifs and medieval numbers.

All alphabets are not the same
Although most European alphabets are Latin based they are not all the same, as some have more letters than others. English has 26 letters, while traditional Spanish has 30 with the addition of 'ñ', 'll', 'ch', 'rr'. Italian has only 21 letters, and lacks 'j', 'k', 'w', 'x' and 'y'.

Below
The English modern day alphabet. A set of 52 majuscule and minuscule forms.

ABCDEFGHIJKLMNOPQRSTUVWXYZ

ABCDEFGHILMNOPQRSTUVZ

Above
The modern Italian alphabet lacks the letters 'j', 'k', 'w', 'x' and 'y'.

Accents and stresses

Various accents and stresses, called diacritical marks, have developed over time to provide visual guides to the pronunciation of letters and words by indicating how the letter sound is to be modified. Pictured below are some of the common accents used with the Latin alphabet, which will be discussed on *page 92.*

Acute

Acute accent, from the Latin *acutus*, meaning 'sharp', represents a vowel is close or tense, has a high or rising pitch, that a vowel is long, or that the syllable in which the vowel appears is stressed.

Circumflex

From the Latin *circumflexus*, meaning 'bent around', the circumflex indicates that a vowel has a long sound.

Breve

From the Latin *brevis*, which means 'short', this symbol placed over a vowel indicates that it has a short sound.

Grave

From the Latin *gravis* meaning 'heavy', it is a mark placed above a vowel to indicate stress or special pronunciation.

Diaeresis / Umlaut

Typical in Germanic languages, the umlaut indicates that a vowel sound changes by assimilating the vowel sound of the following syllable. From the German *um*, meaning 'around' or 'alteration', and *laut*, meaning 'sound'.

Tilde

From the medieval Latin *titulus* meaning 'title', a tilde placed over a letter indicates that a more nasal pronunciation is required such as the Spanish 'ñ', that is pronounced like the 'ny' in 'canyon'.

The 0

Modern numbers derive from Arabic characters and their adoption brought the '0' with them. The numerals themselves originated in India and came into use in Arabic around 1000 AD. Common usage in Europe did not occur until the Renaissance period.

Simplification

Modern European digits were created in India in the 6th century or earlier, but were introduced into the West by Arab scholars. As they represent place-based values and have a value for zero, calculations can be performed with relative ease, as adding the numbers (below right) will prove. Another advantage is that numbers of infinite length can be formed, whereas Roman numerals soon meet with limitations.

M	1000
C	50
VI	6
IV	4

Movable type, 1436

This is a piece of movable type for the 'g' character. Many typographical terms originate with the different characteristics of these type blocks. The physical dimensions of the block dictated spacing and made negative spacing impossible, whereas computer technology makes spacing more flexible. While digitised type still adheres to the same conventions of the bounding box (pictured) in terms of measurements, digitisation allows these boxes to overlap, and indeed have negative tracking.

Left
A printer selecting type from a type case. Pictured below are movable type blocks and the measure they will be set in.

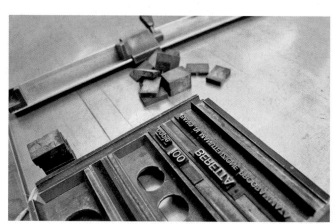

Gutenberg

Johannes Gutenberg (c. 1400–1468) was a German printer who developed the first printing press and the use of movable type. The development of the printing press allowed the mass production of books that previously had to be written by hand. Movable type further improved this development by allowing text characters to be reused, providing further time and cost savings. This technology remained the basis of the printing industry until hot metal printing.

Right
This is a photograph of metal type set in a block that was used by printing presses until well into the 20th century.

Opposite
This is a handwritten vellum from a 1490 edition of the *Book of Hours* prayer book that was used for private devotion from the 12th century. Vellum is a thin sheet of specially prepared leather used for writing, that is superior in quality to parchment.

Blackletter, 1150–1500

Block, Blackletter, Gothic, Old English, black or broken typefaces are based on the ornate writing style prevalent during the Middle Ages. These ornate qualities can be seen in the woodblock letters pictured right. Nowadays these typefaces appear heavy and difficult to read in large text blocks due to the complexity of the letters and the fact that they seem antiquated and unfamiliar to us. Blackletter typefaces are commonly used to add decorative touches such as initial caps and on certificates.

Above
Post-war 100,000 Reichsmark.

Right
Martin Luther's translation of the Bible into German.

Above
This is Blackletter 686, a modern font created by Bitstream Inc. and based on London Text scripts from the Middle Ages that were written with feather quills. The clean lines of this font result in an engraved effect.

Readability

Readability traditionally refers to how well the text is written and prepared, so as to facilitate reading. Readability depends on many factors including the colour of text in relation to its background, spacing, typeface, line length, justification, paragraph density and the grammar used. Increasingly however, readability refers to the impression a piece of text creates. In this context, text set in an illegible typewriter font still conveys a certain readability due to the other elements of its presentation.

Legibility

The ability to distinguish one character from another, to turn letters into words and words into sentences due to qualities inherent in the typeface design is known as legibility.

The effect of printing in Europe

As printing spread it gave rise to various typographical styles with particular hotspots being France, where Blackletter developed, Holland and Italy. Many printers adopted the Venetian model as interest in Italian Renaissance art and culture grew. Parisian printer Claude Garamond (c. 1480–1561) established the first independent type foundry.

Letterforms from this period were more representative of a pen, and utilised the greater detail that working with metal offered.

Old Style typeforms superseded Blackletter as people in Renaissance Europe began to favour classical forms. These are more condensed than the Carolingian forms that preceded them, but rounder and more expanded than Blackletter. These fonts have low contrast, with diagonal stress and serifs with rounded brackets. Many of these fonts feature redrawn characters based on those used in earlier times. For example, Caslon is a font that was redrawn to give a romanticised impression of the characters it is based on.

Above
A book printed and published in the 16th century.

Above
This is a detail from a ca. 16th-century Latin law manuscript printed in Paris. Notice how the ink fills in, probably due to the porosity of the paper stock. The characters therefore needed to be cut to remain legible at small sizes, even with ink spread. The same principle is still used in newspaper faces, *see page 110.*

Above
This is a detail from *De La Cosmographie* by Johannes Kepler (1571–1630). The shapes of the characters are exaggerated to compensate for the deficiencies of the printing process and paper stock so that they remain readable.

ABCDEFGHIJKLMNOPQRSTUVWXYZ

Bembo

Created by Monotype in 1929 for a Stanley Morison project, Bembo is an Old Style font based on a Roman face cut by Francisco Griffo da Bologna, which Aldus Manutius used to print Pietro Bembo's 1496 publication of *De Aetna*. Morison modified letterforms such as the 'G' to create a typeface with 31 weights – an all-purpose font family suitable for almost any application. Note the crossed strokes in the 'W'.

ABCDEFGHIJKLMNOPQRSTUVWXYZ

Garamond

Based on designs by 17th-century French printer Jean Jannon that were themselves based on typefaces cut by Claude Garamond from the 16th century, Garamond is an Aldine font (fonts based on the designs of Aldus Manutius in the 15th century, of which Bembo and Garamond are examples of) that is elegant and readable. Note the crossed strokes in the 'W', and the bowl of the 'P' that does not reach the stem.

ABCDEFGHIJKLMNOPQRSTUVWXYZ

Janson

Created c. 1685 by Hungarian punchcutter Miklós Kis, Janson wrongly bears the name of Dutch punchcutter Anton Janson to whom it was formerly attributed. The font has sturdy forms, strong stroke contrast and is used for book and magazine text. Note the long tail of the 'Q', the oval shape of the 'O' and the unified apex of the 'W'.

ABCDEFGHIJKLMNOPQRSTUVWXYZ

Caslon Antique

This is a modern font based on a historical font. Modern typographers' attempts to recreate ancient fonts in digital format often involve imaginative leaps, as they are based on printed texts where there is ink spread, and in many cases the original fonts are not available to work from.

ABCDEFGHIJKLMNOPQRSTUVWXYZ *vw*

Caslon

Created in 1725 by typographer William Caslon, this serif font was styled on 17th-century Dutch designs. The font can be identified as most Caslons have a capital 'A' with a scooped-out apex, a capital 'C' with two full serifs, and in the italic, a swashed lowercase 'v' and 'w'. The font was chosen by Benjamin Franklin for the first printing of the American Declaration of Independence and has become a popular serif font with versions now provided by numerous type foundries.

ABCDEFGHIJKLMNOPQRSTUVWXYZ

Baskerville

Created by John Baskerville in the 18th century, Baskerville is a versatile transitional font (making it a precursor to the modern faces that followed) with high contrast forms that are used for both body text and display type. Note the absence of the middle serif on the 'W' and the distinctive capital 'Q'.

The Industrial Revolution, 1800s

The Industrial Revolution brought mechanisation that allowed printing to speed up, photo-engraving which replaced handmade printing plates and line-casting machines that revolutionised typesetting and allowed for ever-increasing levels of detail and intricacy. The use of points as the measurement system was cemented during this period.

Technological development also meant that font creation took less time, which opened the doors for the development of a wider range of typefaces and also made extending font families easier. One development of the time was the introduction of **BOLDFACE**. Experimentation with serifs saw them become thinner and thinner until they ultimately disappeared. William Caslon's great grandson William Caslon IV cut the first sans serif font in 1816, called English Egyptian. The absence of serifs was so unusual that other typographers called it grotesque, a name that has stuck and is still used to describe some sans serif fonts. Transitional fonts from this period typically have vertical stress and more contrast than Old Style typefaces, in addition to horizontal serifs. Towards the end of the Industrial Revolution, transitional types began to adopt the characteristics that are seen in modern typefaces.

Pantographic punchcutter, 1885
The pantographic punchcutter, invented by Linn Boyd Benton in 1885, made possible the manufacture of composing machines. As an operator traced a brass pattern of a letter with one part of the device, its cutting tool engraved the letter on to the punch.

Line-casting machine, 1884
Invented by Ottmar Mergenthaler in 1884, the line-casting machine produces a metal slug with a single line of type, with characters input with a keyboard like a typewriter. The machine assembles brass matrices into a line, which it then casts.

American Typefounder ATF, 1892
The merger of 23 type foundries to form American Type Founders Company created what would become the largest type foundry in the world with a monopoly on the type industry until movable type became obsolete.

The Rosetta Stone
The Rosetta Stone (exhibited in the British Museum, London) was carved in 196 BC with an inscription in Egyptian hieroglyphs, demotic and Greek that was found near Rosetta (Rashid) in 1799. The three scripts of the same text provided a valuable key that helped to decipher hieroglyphs.

DISPLAY FACES

GROTESQUE

The first sans serif typeface, 1816
William Caslon developed a sans serif typeface called Egyptian in reference to public interest in Egypt following Napoleon campaign. It was not well received, however, and was called 'grotesque' and 'Gothic' (a style of architecture going through a revival at the time). Egyptian has since come to refer to slab serif typefaces, perhaps because the slabs mirror the construction of the pyramids.

Gothic

The Notre Dame cathedral in Paris, completed in 1250, is considered the foremost example of Gothic architecture, which is characterised by slender vertical piers, counterbalancing buttresses, vaulting and pointed arches.

EGYPTIAN

Commercial art

Lithography was invented in Austria by Alois Senefelder in 1796. Following refinements, by 1848 the process had been refined to print speeds of 10,000 sheets per hour, which made mass production of designs economically viable. Lithography allowed the merging of art with industry to produce posters and colour plates for books. The first person to mass produce posters with lithography was Jules Chéret (1836-1933) in Paris. Other early protagonists include Thomas Theodor Heine (1867-1948) and Henri de Toulouse-Lautrec (1864-1901). Despite these developments, the term 'graphic design' does not appear until the 1950s.

Monotype character caster, 1893

The revolutionary monotype caster cast single letters in lead and composed them into a page. This allowed corrections to be made at the character level rather than having to recast a whole line with linotype. Monotype could also produce leads and quads for spacing. Spacing is explained on *page 95*.

Simplicissimus, 1896 (right)
Thomas Theodor Heine created this illustration for the cover of the German satirical magazine *Simplicissimus* that he co-founded in 1895.

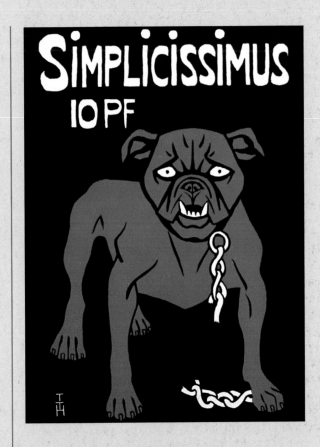

The Chieftains by F.C. Burnand and Arthur Sullivan, 1895
The oversized terminals (T, F, E) and cross bars (H) are used for dramatic effect in this lithograph poster.

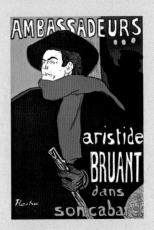

Aristide Bruant at Les Ambassadeurs, Toulouse-Lautrec, 1892
The 'painted' letterforms in this lithograph poster create a singular form combining text and image.

Ninth Almanac, 1904
Distinctive letterforms are rendered, creating a logotype rather than a title in this lithograph poster.

Poster for an Airshow, 1913
Typography mirrors subject matter in this lithograph poster. The rounded 'moderne' structures of the Zeppelin are transposed on to the typography.

Arts and Crafts Movement, 1850s

The Victorian Arts and Crafts Movement developed as a rejection of heavily ornamented interiors with many pieces of furniture, collections of ornamental objects and surfaces covered with fringed cloths. The Arts and Crafts Movement favoured simplicity, and good craftsmanship and design.

British artist and architect William Morris was a leading exponent of this new style that sought to re-establish a link between beautiful work and the worker, by rediscovering an honesty in design that is not found in mass-produced items.

ABCDEFGHIJKLMNOPQRSTUVWXYZ abcdefghijklmnopqrstuvwxyz 1234567890

Cheltenham, Bertram Goodhue, 1896
Originally created by Bertram Grosvenor Goodhue for the Cheltenham Press, New York, this is a serif font that was stronger in appearance than the popular text types of the time, aided by a large x-height that adds to its legibility.

ABCDEFGHIJKLMNOPQRSTUVWXYZ abcdefghijklmnopqrstuvwxyz 1234567890

Franklin Gothic, Morris Fuller Benton, 1904
Designed for American Type Founders, this Gothic or grotesque font gives a dark, monotone look. It has subtle stroke contrast, with the thinning of round strokes as they merge into stems. The font includes a two-story 'g'. Its various weights give it a lot of versatility, making it ideal for newspapers.

ABCDEFGHIJKLMNOPQRSTUVWXYZ abcdefghijklmnopqrstuvwxyz 1234567890

Century Schoolbook, Morris Fuller Benton, 1901
Based on his father's Century font, Morris Fuller Benton made other versions including Century Schoolbook in about 1919. It is round, open and sturdy. Although heavier in appearance than many other serif fonts, it is very legible.

ABCDEFGHIJKLMNOPQRSTUVWXYZ abcdefghijklmnopqrstuvwxyz 1234567890

Century, Linn Boyd Benton, 1906
Based on an original 1894 design by Linn Boyd Benton (father of influential type designer Morris Fuller Benton) for periodical *Century Magazine*, with thin characters to fit tight columns. It is an extremely legible font that is suitable for textbooks, magazines and other publications.

ABCDEFGHIJKLMNOPQRSTUVWXYZ ABCDEFGHIJKLMNOPQRSTUVWXYZ 1234567890

Copperplate Gothic, Frederic Goudy, 1905
Originally created by Frederic Goudy, successive weights were drawn by Clarence Marder for American Type Founders. It is a wide, rather square, monotone Gothic with small hairline serifs reminiscent of the edges on letters that were engraved in copperplate. The characters impart a feel of serious business that is understated and refined. Wide and open, it is legible at small sizes.

ABCDEFGHIJKLMNOPQRSTUVWXYZ abcdefghijklmnopqrstuvwxyz 1234567890

Goudy Old Style, Frederic Goudy, 1910
Inspired by lettering on a Renaissance painting, Goudy Old Style forms the basis for a large family of variants. Highlights include the upward pointing ear of the g, the diamond-shaped dots over the i and j, and the rounded upward swelling of the horizontal strokes at the base of the 'E' and 'L'.

Penny Black, 1840
The world's first postage stamp, the Penny Black, was issued in 1840. The letters in the bottom left and right hand corners denote the stamp's position on the printed sheet, AA, AB, AC etc.

Royal Albert Hall, 1870
In 1870, Queen Victoria opened the Royal Albert Hall in London. The terracotta frieze running the circumference depicts 'The Triumph of the Arts and Sciences'.

ITC RENNIE MACKINTOSH WAS DESIGNED IN 1996 BY PHILL GRIMSHAW FOLLOWING RESEARCH AND COLLABORATION BETWEEN THE INTERNATIONAL TYPEFACE CORP AND GLASGOW SCHOOL OF ART. THE LETTERFORMS ARE BASED ON THE HANDWRITING AND DRAWINGS OF SCOTTISH DESIGNER CHARLES RENNIE MACKINTOSH, WHO PRODUCED HIGHLY ORIGINAL BUILDINGS, INTERIORS AND FURNITURE AT THE TURN OF THE 20TH CENTURY. THE FONT FAMILY IS UNUSUAL AND OFF BEAT, AND A GOOD CHOICE FOR PRODUCT PACKAGING, ADVERTISING, AND GRAPHIC DESIGNS WITH A PERIOD FLAIR.

Rennie Mackintosh, Phill Grimshaw, 1996
The letterforms of Rennie Mackintosh are based on the handwriting and drawings of Scottish designer Charles Rennie Mackintosh.

THE ECKMANN FONT FAMILY IS NAMED AFTER DESIGNER OTTO ECKMANN. WITH A CLEAR JUGENDSTIL INFLUENCE THROUGH THE FLOWING FLORAL CONTOURS, THIS FONT WAS MADE FOR LARGER POINT SIZES FOR USE ON POSTERS. WHILE RELATIVELY LEGIBLE, IT IS NOT MEANT FOR SMALLER PRINT. ECKMANN IS OFTEN USED TO GIVE A NOSTALGIC FEELING.

Eckmann, Otto Eckmann, 1900
Named after designer Otto Eckmann, the characters have flowing floral contours that provide a nostalgic feeling. The typeface was intended for display at large sizes.

Franklin Gothic
Benjamin Franklin, after whom Franklin Gothic was named. Morris Fuller Benton's design of 1904 is still popular today, appearing in many newspapers and as a headline typeface for advertising.

Copperplate Gothic
Copperplate Gothic exhibits some of the attention to detail found in the Arts and Crafts Movement.

Modernism, 1910

Modernism through the cubist, surrealist and Dadaist movements was shaped by the industrialisation and urbanisation of Western society. Modernists departed from the rural and provincial zeitgeist prevalent in the Victorian era, rejecting its values and styles in favour of cosmopolitanism. Functionality and progress became key concerns in the attempt to move beyond the external physical representation of reality through experimentation in a struggle to define what should be considered 'modern'. Modernist typefaces often sought to force viewers to see the everyday differently by presenting unfamiliar forms.

Left
Modernist tendencies can be seen in *Portrait of Béatrice Hastings* by Italian painter and sculptor Amedeo Modigliani that features the deliberate distortion of features and the use of large areas of flat colour.

A RECREATION OF THE ROMAN TYPE CUT BY NICOLAS JENSON IN THE 15TH CENTURY, ROGERS WAS COMMISSIONED TO DESIGN AN EXCLUSIVE TYPE FOR NEW YORK'S METROPOLITAN MUSEUM OF ART. NAMED AFTER *THE CENTAUR*, THE TITLE OF A BOOK BY MAURICE DE GUÉRIN WAS THE FIRST DESIGNED USING THE TYPE.

Centaur, Bruce Rogers, 1914
American Bruce Rogers created this font for New York's Metropolitan Museum of Art based on Nicolas Jenson's 15th-century recreation of Roman type. It is named after *The Centaur* by Maurice de Guérin, the first book to use the font.

Above
The Pompidou arts centre in Paris, created by Renzo Piano and Richard Rogers in 1977. It is a modernist building that follows the mantra of 'form follows function', and its aesthetics are integral to its function.

De Stijl, 1917
An art and design movement founded around the magazine of the same name that was founded by Theo Van Doesburg. De Stijl used strong rectangular forms, employed primary colours and celebrated asymmetrical compositions.

Constructivism, 1918
A modern art movement originating in Moscow in 1920, characterised by the use of industrial materials such as glass, sheet metal and plastic to create non representational, often geometric objects. Russian constructivism was influential to modernism through its use of black and red sans serif typography arranged in asymmetrical blocks.

LONDON UNDERGROUND IS A SANS SERIF DEVELOPED BY EDWARD JOHNSTON FOR THE LONDON UNDERGROUND SYSTEM IN 1916, CHARACTERISED BY WIDE, ROUNDED CHARACTERS WITH AN EVEN STROKE WEIGHT THAT GIVES HIGH LEGIBILITY.

Johnston Underground, Edward Johnston, 1916

This striking sans serif font was created by Edward Johnston for use on the signage of the London Underground. Originally called Underground, it has also been called Johnston's Railway Type and Johnston. Typographer Eric Gill studied under Johnston, who is considered the father of the 20th century typography revival, and this connection is clear to see in Gill Sans, which further refines the London Underground font. Gill Sans has more classical proportions, geometric elements and contains a distinctive capital 'R' and eyeglass lowercase 'g'.

GILL SANS FURTHER REFINES THE SIMPLE LINES OF JOHNSTON'S ORIGINAL FONT.

The Bauhaus, 1919

The Bauhaus opened in 1919 under the direction of renowned architect Walter Gropius. Until forced to close in 1933, the Bauhaus sought to initiate a fresh approach to design following the First World War, with a focus on functionality rather than adornment.

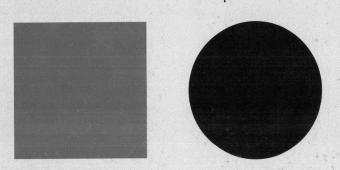

Left

In 1923 Russian Wassily Kandinsky, a tutor on the Bauhaus Basic Course, proposed that there was a universal relationship between the three basic shapes and the three primary colours, with the yellow triangle being the most active and dynamic, through to the passive, cold blue circle.

Dadaism, 1916-1923

An artistic and literary movement (1916—23) that developed following World War I and sought to discover an authentic reality through the abolition of traditional culture and aesthetic forms. Dadaism brought new ideas, materials and directions, but with little uniformity. Its principles were of deliberate irrationality, anarchy and cynicism, and the rejection of laws of beauty. Dadaists lived in the moment and for the moment.

Dada, Richard Kegler, 1995-1998
Inspired by Dada typography and poetry, Richard Kegler created Dada according to the principles of irrationality and anarchic arrangement so that there appears to be little congruence from one letter to the next.

Bayer Universal (top), Bayer Fonetik (bottom), Herbert Bayer, 1925
Herbert Bayer embodied the modernist desire to reduce designs to as few elements as possible and repeatedly experimented with typography to reduce the alphabet to a single case.

bayer universal
BAYER fonetik

Basic Alphabet (below) was a further experimentation with language, with words written like they sound, and with silent letters dropped. The letterforms in some way try to visually express the sounds they represent, as typographical elements are reduced. Capitals are indicated with an underscore for example.

basik Alfabet

kabel
KABEL

ITC Kabel, Victor Caruso, 1976
Kabel features basic forms influenced by stone-carved Roman letters that consist of a few pure and clear geometric forms such as circles, squares and triangles. Art Deco elements such as the seemingly awkward angles of some of the curves makes Kabel appear very different from other geometric modernist typefaces. Based on an earlier design by Rudolph Koch in 1923.

ABCDEFGHIJKLMNOPQRSTUVWXYZ
abcdefghijklmnopqrstuvwxyz 1234567890

Perpetua, Eric Gill, 1928
Eric Gill based this design on the characters from old engravings. Small diagonal serifs and a medieval number set add an element of formality to the typeface.

ABCDEFGHIJKLMNOPQRSTUVWXYZ
abcdefghijklmnopqrstuvwxyz 1234567890

Gill Sans, Eric Gill, 1930
Taught by Edward Johnston, who designed the London Underground signage, Eric Gill gave Gill Sans more classical proportions than Johnston's design. He included a flared capital 'R' and eyeglass lowercase 'g' in this humanist sans serif that has geometric touches.

futura *Script*

BODONI POSTER BOLDFACE

Futura, Paul Renner, 1928

Futura is considered the major typeface development to come out of the constructivist orientation of the Bauhaus movement. Typographer Paul Renner based the characters on the simple forms of circle, triangle and square, but softened them to be more legible and to create a new, modern type that was more than an old revival. The long elegant ascenders and descenders benefit from generous line spacing and help create this striking and radical typeface that is strong and elegant.

Poster Bodoni, Chauncey H. Griffith, 1929

Based on an 18th century design by Gianbattista Bodoni, this is a modern font characterised by hairline serifs that are subtly bracketed and heavy downstrokes that give a powerful vertical stress.

Nazi Germany, 1931

The dictatorship of Adolf Hitler promised Germany *Ein Volk, ein Reich, ein Führer!* (One people, one empire, one leader!), a message dramatically reinforced through the visual arts. The Nazi regime actively promoted Blackletter type as the official type-style for Germany, linking it with a nostalgic idea of German culture, until 1941 when Blackletter was outlawed in favour of Roman type. The Nazis also liked the modern, industrial look of Bauhaus typefaces, which they endorsed in the 1940s, when it was thought that a Roman typeface would have more international appeal.

Barcelona Pavilion, Ludwig Mies van der Rohe, built 1928-1929, demolished 1930

This steel frame, glass and polished stone building was emblematic of the modern movement. The original use of materials expressed the ideal of modernity through its geometry, the precision of the pieces constructed and the clarity of their assembly.

The Second World War, 1939-1945

A global war in which Great Britain, France, the Soviet Union, the United States, China, and other allies defeated Germany, Italy, and Japan. Designs created under both forces were geared towards propaganda and featured symbolic and/or heroic images to help their respective war efforts. One of the effects of this war was the displacement of designers, architects and other creatives from Europe to the USA.

1950s

Following the Second World War a new optimism emerged as a consumer boom erupted in the USA. The cultural scene also expanded, boosted by many European creatives and intellectuals who had fled Nazi Europe, and the teenager emerged as both a market and creative force. Design became more elaborate, with bright colours that celebrated life – as personified in cars such as the candy-coloured *Ford Thunderbird*. The demand for wider choice and the emergence of photosetting helped typography develop. Typographers such as Hermann Zapf led the humanist movement, with the lines between serif and sans serif typefaces blurred as organic lines were reintroduced into typography. Humanist fonts have forms that are based on classic Romans, but without the serifs.

Ford Thunderbird
Launched in 1955, the *Thunderbird* is the quintessential 1950s two-seat convertible American car that defined the luxury car market.

Helvetica, Max Miedinger, 1957
Created by Max Miedinger - the forgotten designer - Helvetica is one of the most famous and popular typefaces in the world. With clean, no-nonsense shapes based on the Akzidenz-Grotesk font. Originally called Haas Grotesk, its name changed to Helvetica in 1960. The Helvetica family has 34 weights and the Neue Helvetica has 51.

ABCDEFGHIJKLMNOPQRSTUVWXYZ
abcdefghijklmnopqrstuvwxyz 1234567890

Univers, Adrian Frutiger, 1957
With sturdy, clean forms Univers expresses cool elegance and rational competence. It is available in 59 weights that combine well with other fonts.

ABCDEFGHIJKLMNOPQRSTUVWXYZ
abcdefghijklmnopqrstuvwxyz 1234567890

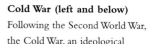

Pictured in black is Helvetica and in magenta is Univers. Although both are sans serif fonts, there are noticeable differences such as the absence of a tail on the Univers 'G', 'y' and 'a', the more open, rounded counter on the Univers 'a' and the bisecting tail of the Helvetica 'Q'.

Cold War (left and below)
Following the Second World War, the Cold War, an ideological conflict, developed between the USA and the USSR. This was characterised by intense distrust, the build upof nuclear weapons and geo-political manoeuvering.

Guggenheim (left)
One of the world's leading modern art museums, the Solomon R. Guggenheim Museum was founded in New York City in 1939 and noted for the spiral building designed by architect Frank Lloyd Wright and opened in 1959.

ABCDEFGHIJKLMNOPQRSTUVWXYZ abcdefghijklmnopqrstuvwxyz 1234567890

Palatino, Hermann Zapf, 1950
Named after Giambattista Palatino, a master of calligraphy from the days of Leonardo da Vinci, Palatino is a universally admired Zapf typeface. It is optimised for legibility, with open counters and carefully weighted strokes based on classical Italian Renaissance forms that were legible even on the inferior quality papers available following the Second World War.

ABCDEFGHIJKLMNOPQRSTUVWXYZ abcdefghijklmnopqrstuvwxyz 1234567890

Melior, Hermann Zapf, 1952
Melior was designed as a newspaper face with short ascenders and descenders, specifically for letterpress and offset printing. It has a robust character with classic and objective forms, and is versatile and extremely legible.

based on handwriting

Mistral, Roger Excoffon, 1953
A loose running script based on the handwriting of typographer Roger Excoffon, who wanted to create a typeface with the variety and non-uniformity of handwriting.

Santa Croce
Santa Croce, completed in 1442, is the largest Franciscan church in Florence in the simple basilica style, with a nave and two isles.

THE GOLDEN RATIO

Optima, Hermann Zapf, 1958
Optima was inspired by letters Zapf sketched on two 1,000 lire bank notes, based on grave plates cut c. 1530 that he saw while visiting the Santa Croce church in Florence. Optima is a humanist sans serif blended with Roman and calligraphic styles, making it a smooth read and general purpose font, which became his most successful typeface. Letterforms are in the proportions of the golden ratio. The golden ratio is discussed on *pages 68*.

International Style (Swiss)
International or Swiss Style was based on the revolutionary principles of the 1920s such as De Stijl, Bauhaus and Jan Tschichold's *The New Typography* that became firmly established in the 1950s. Grids, mathematical principles, minimal decoration and sans serif typography became the norm as typography developed to represent universal usefulness more than personal expression.

Jan Tschichold, 1902-1974
Jan Tschichold's *Die Neue Typographie (The New Typography)*, published in 1928, expounded the idea of simplicity, clarity and functionality, sans serif fonts and asymmetry. Tschichold was driven by the desire to make efficient use of materials to result in a fairer world, such as doing away with uppercase characters. Escaping Nazi Germany to Switzerland, he later recanted some of his earlier prescriptive ideas, feeling they were too similar to the thought control of Nazism and Stalinism.

Asymmetrical
An asymmetrical layout features a grid that is the same on both the recto and verso pages, and typically has a bias towards one side of the page. In the illustration above, the grid is biased towards the right.

1960s

The world of culture went pop in the 1960s as music, art, literature and furniture design became more accessible and reflected elements of everyday life.

Pop art

Pop art developed as a reaction against abstract art. It was often witty, purposely obvious and throwaway in its reflection of consumer culture such as advertising and comic books. Pop art's influence on typography resulted in fonts – particularly for display type – designed or selected according to possible associations or references in place of any particular theory regarding legibility or aesthetics, while the International Style remained influential for body text.

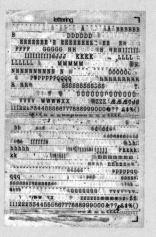

Letraset, 1961
The creation of Letraset dry-transfer lettering allowed anyone to do typesetting. Easily rubbed directly on to artwork or virtually any substrate, it was often used for headlines and display type while body type was supplied via a typewriter. Letraset commissioned new typefaces including Colin Brignall's futuristic Countdown font (below).

Countdown, Colin Brignall, 1965
This typeface developed for Letraset is synonymous with the 1960s, the space race and the development of computer technology.

DISPLAY

Davida, Louis Minott, 1965
Display typeface designed for the Visual Graphics Corporation.

Body text

Letter Gothic,
Roger Roberson, 1962
Originally designed for use on an IBM Selectric typewriter

Psychedelia

Towards the end of the decade the anti-establishment hippy movement and 'flower power' counterculture saw increasing use of text and artwork with a strong art nouveau influence that provided a visual simile of the effect of psychedelic drugs, with distorted text and colours that challenged conventional readability.

Volkswagen Kombi 1950
The Volkswagen Kombi was launched in 1950 and based on a 1947 sketch by Dutch distributor Ben Pon. Although the millionth Kombi was sold in 1961, it is most associated with the hippy movement later that decade.

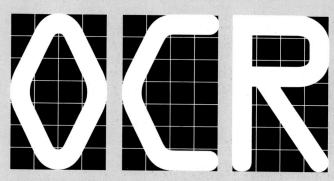

OCR-A, Optical Character Recognition, Adrian Frutiger and the USA Bureau of Standards, 1966
OCR-A is a standardised, monospaced font designed for Optical Character Recognition by electronic devices, using standards developed by the American National Standards Institute in 1966 for the processing of documents by banks and credit card companies. The characters fit into a 4 x 7 grid which makes them easily read by a scanner, even though they are not so legible to the human eye. Subsequent version OCR-B was made a world standard in 1973 and is more legible to the human eye.

Eurostile, Aldo Novarese, 1962

Eurostile features a subtle distortion of circular sans serif geometric forms, with rounded corners that look like television sets. Created by Italian typographer Aldo Novarese, it reflects the zeitgeist of the 1950s and 1960s, giving text a dynamic, modern feel. Eurostile gives text a technological aura that works well for headlines and small bodies of text.

Eurostile

ABCDEFGHIJKLMNOPQRSTUVWXYZ
abcdefghijklmnopqrstuvwxyz 1234567890

ABCDEFGHIJKLMNOPQRSTUVWXYZ
abcdefghijklmnopqrstuvwxyz 1234567890

ABCDEFGHIJKLMNOPQRSTUVWXYZ
abcdefghijklmnopqrstuvwxyz 1234567890

ABCDEFGHIJKLMNOPQRSTUVWXYZ
abcdefghijklmnopqrstuvwxyz 1234567890

ABCDEFGHIJKLMNOPQRSTUVWXYZ
abcdefghijklmnopqrstuvwxyz 1234567890

Syntax, Hans E. Meier, 1968

Syntax is a humanist monoline (a typeface with a uniform stroke width) sans serif based on Renaissance letterforms.

AACHEN

COLIN BRIGNALL DESIGNED AACHEN FOR LETRASET IN 1969 AS A TITLE FONT. IT HAS STRONG, CONCISE CHARACTERS THAT STAND OUT. AACHEN IS A BRACKETED SLAB SERIF DESIGN. FOR MORE INFORMATION ON TYPES OF SERIFS, SEE PAGES 86–87.

1970s

Typography in the 1970s continued where the 1960s left off, becoming more decorative, outrageous and extravagant until the middle of the decade, when punk emerged. Punk rejected the decadent, elaborate nature of music, fashion and the visual arts in favour of the disposable and shocking.

ITC, 1970s

The International Typeface Corp. (ITC) was formed in New York to market new typeface designs, distribute royalties to the creators and extend rights to typographers that were threatened by the photographic copying of fonts. Prior to this, type designers had been tied to particular typesetting machine manufacturers. The formation of the ITC resulted in a drive to collect and commission new work, including revisiting classic fonts.

Anarchy symbol
The circled A is an anarchist symbol popularised by the 1970s punk movement, although it dates back to the anarchist militia in the Spanish Civil War of the 1930s.

austrian designer michael neugebauer created cirkulus in 1970 as an experimental display face using combinations of hairline circles and straight lines. the letters have a constructivist feel that is reminiscent of the revolutionary 1920s. cirkulus is a unicase alphabet, with a very lightweight appearance that is best used in large display sizes.

Early computers and photocomposition, 1970s

Photocomposition improved in the 1960s and facilitated the copying and production of fonts. By projecting a character created on the screen of a cathode ray tube (like a TV) through a lens on to light-sensitive paper or film, it could be stored in a magnetic memory, overwritten and edited. This was much faster than physically adjusting hot metal type and led to increased proliferation of typefaces and historical revivals as fonts became more international. The 1970s saw computers increasingly involved in this process through a mixture of photocomposition and the digital techniques that would emerge later, with several competing languages and formats. Throughout this decade the potential to design directly on screen increased, offering industry professionals more options and flexibility.

Avant Garde, Herb Lubalin and Tom Carnase, 1970
Designed by Herb Lubalin and Tom Carnase and based on Lubalin's logo for *Avant Garde* magazine, this is a geometric sans serif type reminiscent of the work from the 1920s German Bauhaus movement, whose geometric shapes were made with a compass and T-square. The large, open counters and tall x-heights seem friendly, and help to make this family effective for headlines and short texts.

ABCDEFGHIJKLMNOPQRSTUVWXYZ
abcdefghijklmnopqrstuvwxyz 1234567890

ITC Souvenir, Ed Benguiat, 1970
Type designer and calligrapher Ed Benguiat produced several fonts for ITC including ITC Souvenir (1972), ITC Bauhaus (1975) and ITC Benguiat (1977). Benguiat was influential in the revival of art nouveau typefaces and created logotypes for *The New York Times*, *Playboy* and *Readers' Digest*.

ABCDEFGHIJKLMNOPQRSTUVWXYZ
abcdefghijklmnopqrstuvwxyz 1234567890

ITC Cheltenham, Tony Stan, 1978
Originally designed by Bertram Goodhue, it was expanded by Morris Fuller Benton and completed by Stan in 1975 with a larger x-height and improved italic details.

ABCDEFGHIJKLMNOPQRSTUVWXYZ
abcdefghijklmnopqrstuvwxyz 1234567890

ITC Bauhaus, Ed Benguiat, 1975
Based on a prototype face drawn by Herbert Bayer in 1925, ITC Bauhaus has simple geometric shapes and monotone stroke weights with rounded, open forms and quirky geometric gyrations.

ABCDEFGHIJKLMNOPQRSTUVWXYZ
abcdefghijklmnopqrstuvwxyz 1234567890

Frutiger, Adrian Frutiger, 1976
Adrian Frutiger expanded and completed the family of typefaces he began in 1968 while designing signage for the Charles de Gaulle airport in Paris.

ABCDEFGHIJKLMNOPQRSTUVWXYZ
abcdefghijklmnopqrstuvwxyz 1234567890

ITC Garamond, Tony Stan, 1977
Loosely based on the forms of the original 16th century Garamond, this version has a taller x-height and tighter letterspacing, making it suitable for advertising or packaging, manuals and handbooks.

ABCDEFGHIJKLMNOPQRSTUVWXYZ
abcdefghijklmnopqrstuvwxyz 1234567890

ITC Benguiat, Ed Benguiat, 1977
Named after its New York designer Edward Benguiat, this art nouveau design has slight curves in diagonals, and crossbars where straight strokes would be expected.

STOP IS A FUTURISTIC SANS SERIF DISPLAY FONT CHARACTERISTIC OF THE SUPERSONIC AGE, WITH VAGUELY STENCIL-LIKE LETTERFORMS. SOME CHARACTERS ONLY READ AS LETTERS WHEN USED IN COMBINATION WITH OTHER CHARACTERS.

Stop, Aldo Novarese, 1971 (above)
A stencil-inspired futuristic font, Stop displays the preoccupation of the time. Themes of supersonic travel and geometric reduction create an unmistakable and characterful letterform.

Concorde, 1976 (left)
An iconic, delta-winged supersonic passenger aircraft developed by Aérospatiale-BAC that entered service in 1976 and had a cruising speed of Mach 2.02 (1,540 mph).

1980s

The 1980s saw the introduction of personal computers, computer games, music videos and desktop publishing, as the invention of the laser printer meant that expensive photosensitive paper was no longer needed. As hairstyles and shoulder pads got bigger and bigger, physical cutting and pasting in graphic design was eliminated as computers took over, giving greater ability to experiment. The digital revolution meant that new fonts could be designed and trialled quickly and easily, without the great expense and commitment of hot metal type.

Arial is a contemporary sans serif design that contains many humanist characteristics. The overall treatment of curves is softer and fuller than in most industrial style sans serif faces. Terminal strokes are cut on the diagonal and help to give the face a less mechanical appearance. Arial is a versatile family that can be used with equal success in many different applications.

Arial Black, Robin Nicholas and Patricia Saunders, 1982

Bitstream, 1981

Bitstream, founded in 1981 by Matthew Carter and Mike Parker, was the the first digital type foundry. The production of digital fonts further separated type design from manufacturers. Bitsream developed Charter with open letterforms for low-resolution printers and created Verdana for screen use, with curves, diagonals and straight lines rendered in pixel patterns, rather than drawn.

open letterforms

Charter, Matthew Carter, 1993

A traditional Old Style typeface, Charter was designed as a highly legible text typeface for use on both laser writers and high-resolution image setters.

Verdana

Verdana, Matthew Carter, 1996

Verdana is a sans serif font commissioned by software firm Microsoft specifically to address the challenges of on-screen display. The font is stripped of features that are redundant on screen. Its characteristics are derived from pixel rather than the pen, with weighting that ensures that pixel patterns at small sizes are pleasing, clear and legible.

The Face, 1981–2004

Graphic designer Neville Brody revolutionised magazine design with his unabashed love of typography that he displayed on the pages of *The Face*, a style magazine covering music, design and fashion. Historic and contemporary type were subjected to exaggeration in scale and proportion, were exploded and otherwise distorted, and complemented with Brody's own computer-generated fonts as he challenged the notion of legibility.

Postmodernism

Following the Second World War, postmodernism questioned the notion that there is a reliable reality by deconstructing authority and the established order through fragmentation, incoherence and the plain ridiculous. Postmodernism returned to earlier ideas of adornment and decoration, celebrating expression and personal intuition rather than dogmatic formulae and structure. Designers turned to vernacular design, such as Barry Decks' Template Gothic (inspired by a launderette sign), rather than seeking universal truths.

Template Gothic - a vernacular typeface

Template Gothic, Barry Deck, 1990

Template Gothic was inspired by a launderette sign made with stencil templates. The design conveys a sense of imperfection and the distorted ravages of photomechanical reproduction that embraces the vernacular of low culture.

The 'Mac', 1984

Macintosh revolutionised the personal computer by making computer screens user-friendly and hiding the operational programming from the user, in contrast to IBM's approach. Control in type production migrated away from professional typesetters to designers, and extended to amateurs as well as industry professionals. The low resolution of early personal computers called for new fonts to ensure legibility.

Fontographer, 1985

Typeface customisation became available to anyone through the advent of the Fontographer design program, which allowed existing fonts to be manipulated and reshaped. Cheap Fontographer-produced fonts entering the market initially caused concerns for traditional typography companies, although this was tempered by the amount of work it takes to create an entirely new typeface.

Haus der Kulturen, 1988

This logo for Haus der Kulturen der Welt (HdKdW), a cultural institute in Berlin, was hand-drawn by design agency Research Studios. As well as providing an identity, the logo was produced with an adaptable colour system that was used to identify the different activities and print requirements of the institute.

ABCDEFGHIJKLMNOPQRSTUVWXYZ
abcdefghijklmnopqrstuvwxyz 1234567890

Citizen, Zuzana Licko, 1986

The Citizen font was inspired by the smooth printing option provided by Macintosh, which processed 72dpi bitmaps into 300dpi bitmaps for laser printers, seemingly polishing stair step pixels into smooth diagonals. Straight line segments were used to approximate the features of smooth printing.

ABCDEFGHIJKLMNOPQRSTUVWXYZ
ABCDEFGHIJKLMNOPQRSTUVWXYZ
ABCDEFGHIJKLMNOPQRSTUVWXYZ
ABCDEFGHIJKLMNOPQRSTUVWXYZ

Stone, Sumner Stone and Bob Ishi, 1987

Sumner Stone developed several fonts while director of typography at Adobe from 1984-1989. Initially selecting fonts from established libraries, he began designing and commissioning typefaces that would maintain legibility at different resolutions. Stone includes a serif and sans-serif with an informal style that is very legible and makes a modern, dynamic impression.

Trixie, LettError, 1989

Trixie is based on the imperfections of a monospaced typewriter font as font design turned again towards developing more sophisticated and smoother fonts. LettError based Trixie on the look of a dirty, inky typewriter type to give a rougher look that is irreverent and playful. Dutch company LettError was established by Dutch designers Erik van Blokland and Just van Rossum.

1990s

As the 1990s began, graphic designers reacted to the International Style and sought to break away from the constraints of the grid patterns in favour of experimentation, playful use of type and a more handmade approach. Type use became more subtle and expressive – to be part of the message rather than just its conveyor.

FUSE, Neville Brody / Research Studios, 1991
Typography magazine *FUSE*, founded by Neville Brody and John Wozencroft, saw typography explode into uncharted realms as type designers grabbed hold of the 'free reins' that computer technology put in their hands and indulged their imaginations to the full.

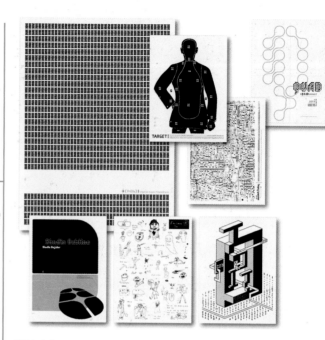

T-26 / Segura Inc., 1994
The explosive growth and power of personal computers and the increasing performance of software has made typeface design easier and given rise to digital type foundries such as T-26, which was established by graphic designer Carlos Segura. Segura believes that some fonts are so decorative that they almost become visuals that tell a story beyond the words.

Indien, Neville Brody / Research Studios, 1991
To avoid the use of Indian typography in a poster for an Indian festival, Neville Brody used a colour system to reflect the life and culture of India and to suggest a modern, dynamic nation with the use of understated Akzidenz Grotesk expanded for the typography.

INDIEN

a pattern of type

Flixel, Just van Rossum / FUSE, 1991
Flixel is a dot pattern font that pushes the boundaries of legibility with its unusual forms.

A font that's a sans **and a serif**

Officina, Erik Spiekermann and MetaDesign, 1990
With both serif and sans serif forms, Officina embodies the ideals of efficient office communication, with styling based on traditional typewriters but adapted to modern technology and spaced to offer optimal legibility.

Designed for low grade printing

Meta, Erik Spiekermann and MetaDesign, 1991
Meta was based on a rejected typeface commissioned by the German Post Office (Bundespost) in 1984. Hailed as the typeface for the 1990s, it is named after Meta Studio, where the new typeface was exclusively used.

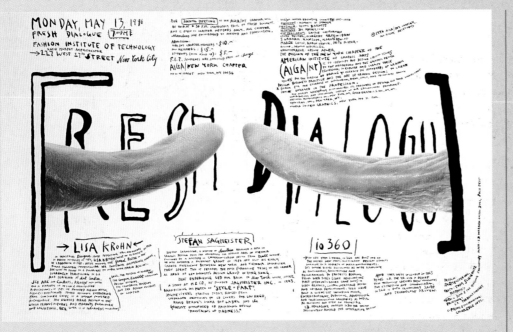

Fresh Dialogue / Stefan Sagmeister, 1996
This poster for the American Institute of Graphic Arts features handwritten typography that is placed in seemingly haphazard blocks. Photos of cow tongues form the crossbars of the capital 'F' of Fresh and reversed 'E' at the end of Dialogue.

Foundry Sans and Foundry Gridnik, 1990 / 1999
Referred to as 'the thinking man's Courier', designer Jürgen Weltin created sans serif characters that use angles rather than curves.

Light
Medium
Bold
Light
Medium
Bold

You can read me, Phil Baines / FUSE, 1995
This typeface uses key portions of letterforms that just about retain legibility.

This is Mrs Eaves, created by typographer Zuzana Licko and named after Sarah Eaves, the woman who typographer John Baskerville married. The font features a series of ligatures that give it a contemporary twist.

Mrs Eaves, Zuzana Licko, 1996
Zuzana Licko created Mrs Eaves based on the design of Baskerville that was originally designed by typographer John Baskerville. Licko gave the font ligatures, such as between the 's' and 't', that give it a contemporary twist. The font is named after Baskerville's housekeeper Sarah Eaves.

Pushkin, Gennady Fridman, 1999
Typography uses references from the past as well as looking to the future to provide the tools for print communication. Pushkin, for example, is based on the autograph of Russian poet Alexander Pushkin (1799–1837), with several versions available that correspond to changes in his orthography.

Graphic design since 2000

High resolution digital printing has increased the options and challenges in graphic design. The growth of multimedia applications presents new demands on fonts, with the need to obtain legibility between computers, mobile phones and other devices. Graphic designers continue to experiment and enjoy the ability that modern technology allows to free-form type quickly and integrate it in their designs.

Pluralism

Today we are living in a pluralistic phase, embracing the ability to move between different styles and points of view. Rather than there being a single meta-narrative, pluralists suggest that there are many narratives and that fewer universal truths exist in a globalised world. Truths are instead more individualistic, personal and specific. This results in regionalism in graphic design, as something that is appropriate in one country will not necessarily translate well in another.

T Bar, George & Vera, 2006
This design for T Bar, a bar-restaurant in the Tea Building in London's Shoreditch, uses eclectic, almost surreal images including typography that looks like line drawings or etchings.

Diesel Fifty book by Vasava Artworks, 2006
These elaborate uppercase letters seem to come from a fantasy novel, but were in fact created by Spain's Vasava Artworks design studio for clothing brand Diesel for its *Fifty* book that gives an insight into the life of Renzo Rosso and the Diesel universe he created. The story of how he evolved from jeans manufacturer to premium brand is told over more than 200 pages and includes subjects such as steps to creativity and cult objects. Creativity is a central theme that permeates the book, as shown in the dramatic style as the cover image (red) and typography. Every spread provides a different creative idea.

Designer as Maker, Studio Myerscough, 2005
Type can be many things. It can be quiet, loud, brash, understated, but ultimately, it can be unexpected. Studio Myerscough, with their freethinking approach to the possibilities of typography, demonstrate the ironic beauty and power of a simple message.

Logotypes, Parent, 2005
Design software applications have made negative tracking a real possibility
for the designer as these logotypes by design studio Parent show. Above,
the type features overly rounded, almost inflated forms that overlap to create
a distinctive identity that is enhanced by the drip effect and colour selection.
Below, the letters work together like a Greek key border, seemingly forming
one continuous string, although each one is separate.

Rock Style, Studio Myerscough, 2005
Studio Myerscough design studio created this dynamic illuminated
typography for an exhibition on rock style. The type installation is
informative and adds style to the event in a way that is denotive, in that
the message tells us that it is about fashion, and cognitive in that the red
Marquee letters suggest fame, fashion and rock music.

A Flock of Words, Why Not Associates and Gordon Young, ongoing
Flock of Words is the result of a six-year collaboration. It features a number
of typographic installations in Morecambe, England as part of a town arts
project that includes poems and traditional sayings.

Museon, Faydherbe / De Vringer, 2006
This is an invitation for an exhibition at Museon museum in The Hague,
the Netherlands, that features the multicolour identity created by Dutch
designers Faydherbe / De Vringer. The structural and modernist approach
is playful and memorable.

2

A discussion of type involves the use
of specific terminology relating to its
historic characteristics and measurement.
An understanding of this terminology
and the measurement system is essential
for the satisfactory communication of
typographical concepts.

a few
basics

This invitation was created
by Turnbull Grey design studio
for private equity firm Bain &
Company. The ascenders have
been extended to appear like the
straws through which the drinks
at the party would be drunk.

Typefaces and fonts

In common usage, the words *typeface* and *font* are used synonymously. In most cases there is no harm in doing so as the substitution is virtually universal and most people, including designers, would be hard pressed to state each word's true definition.

However, each term possesses a separate and distinct meaning. A typeface is a collection of characters which have the same distinct design, while a font is the physical means of typeface production – be it the description of a typeface in computer code, lithographic film or metal. James Felici in his *Complete Manual of Typography* explains the difference as a font being a cookie cutter and the typeface the cookie produced. So while one can ask 'What typeface is that?' or 'What font was used in that publication?', a question such as 'What font is that?' when looking at a piece of print or a screen is inaccurate.

What is a font?
A font is the physical means used to create a typeface, whether it be a typewriter, a stencil, letterpress blocks or a piece of PostScript code.

What is a typeface?
A typeface is a collection of characters, letters, numerals, symbols and punctuation, which have the same distinct design. Pictured below are examples of typefaces produced using the 'cookie cutters' mentioned (left): a typewriter, a stencil, a letterpress and a piece of PostScript code.

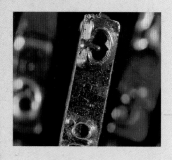

Above
A typewriter produces a distinctive typeface, a stencil produces a rough and ready font, letterpress blocks produce richly expressive type, and a computer font containing PostScript information creates a neat and precise typeface such as Bembo.

Typeface anatomy

Typographical characters have an array of attributes and forms that are described through a variety of different terms, in much the same way as the different names for every part of the human body.

A

Apex
The point formed at the top of a character such as 'A', where the left and right strokes meet.

FY

Arm
A horizontal stroke that is open at one or both ends, as seen on the 'T', and 'F' as well as the upstroke on the 'K' and 'Y'. Also called bar.

b p

Ascenders and descenders
An ascender is the part of a letter that extends above the x-height; a descender falls below the baseline.

GS

Barb
A sharp pointed *serif*.

T

Beak
The *serif* form at the end of an *arm*.

pd

Bowl
The part of a character that encloses a space in circular letterforms such as 'O' and 'e'. The bowl may be closed or open.

T

Bracket
The transitional shape, connecting the *stem* and the *serif*.

G

Chin
The angled *terminal* of a 'G'.

pC

Counter
The space inside a *bowl* as found on 'e', 'a' and other letters.

t

Cross stroke
A horizontal stroke that intersects the central *stem*. Also called a *crossbar*.

A

Crossbar
The horizontal stroke on the characters 'A', 'H', 'T', 'e', 'f', and 't' that intersects the central *stem*. Also called a *cross stroke*.

VK

Crotch
The inner point at which two angled strokes meet.

gr

Ear
A small stroke extending from the right side of the *bowl* of a 'g' or protruding from the *stem* of letters such as 'r' and 'f'.

af

Finial
An ornamental *terminal* stroke at the top of characters such as the 'a' and 'f'.

LR

Leg
The lower, possibly downward sloping stroke of a letter. Sometimes also used for the *tail* of the 'Q'.

ff

Ligature
Typically a *crossbar* or *arm* that extends across a pair of letters to join them.

g

Link
A stroke that joins two other letter parts such as the *bowls* of a double-storey 'g'.

g

Loop
The *bowl* formed by the tail of a double-storey 'g'.

T

Serif
A small stroke at the end of a main vertical or horizontal stroke.

h

Shoulder
The curved stroke leading into the *leg* of an 'h' or 'n' for example.

S

Spine
A left-to-right curving stroke in the 'S' and 's'.

b

Spur
The *terminal* to a *stem* of a rounded letter.

VT

Stem
The main vertical or diagonal stroke of a letter.

Oo

Stress
The orientation, or slant of a curved character.

W

Swash
An elongated curved entry or exit stroke.

Q

Tail
The descending stroke on a 'Q', 'K' and 'R'. The descenders on 'g', 'j', 'p', 'q' and 'y' may also be called *tails*, as can the loop of the 'g'.

T

Terminal
The end of a stroke, which may take several forms such as acute, flared, convex, concave and rounded.

M

Vertex
The angle formed at the bottom of a letter where the left and right strokes meet, such as in the 'M'.

Relative and absolute measurements

Typography uses two types of measurements, *absolute measurements* and *relative measurements*. It is important to understand the differences between these to understand many of the typographic processes.

Absolute measurements

Absolute measurements are easy to understand as they are measurements of fixed values. For example, a millimetre is a precisely defined increment of a centimetre. Equally, points and picas, the basic typographic measurements, have fixed values. All absolute measurements are expressed in finite terms that cannot be altered. Pictured below are four measurement systems that express the same physical distance.

Relative measurements

In typography, many measurements, such as character spacing, are linked to type size, which means that their relationships are defined by a series of relative measurements. Ems and ens for example are relative measurements that have no prescribed, absolute size. Their size is relative to the size of type that is being set.

Leading is another example of the use of relative measurement. Most desktop publishing programs assign an automatic percentage value for functions like leading. The characters below (far left) are 10pt, so with leading set at 120 percent, they are effectively being set on 12pt leading. As the type gets bigger, so does the leading as it is relative to the type size.

If this did not happen and the leading remained constant, as the characters get bigger they would eventually crash into one another, as in the bottom row.

3 inches (3")

76.2 millimetres (76.2mm)

216 points (216pt)

18 picas (18 pica)

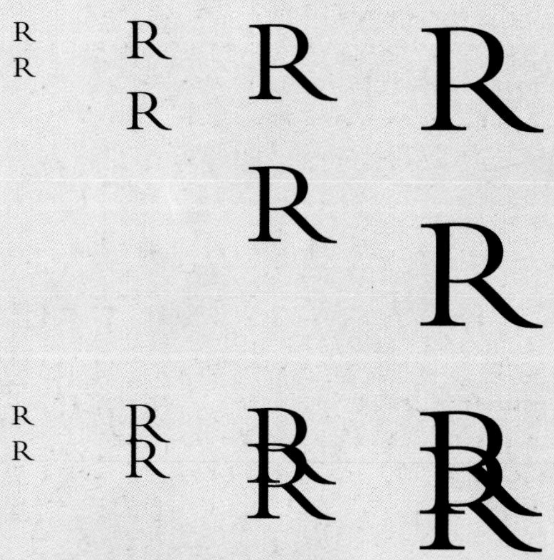

Points

The point is the unit of measurement used to measure the type size of a font, for example, 7pt Times New Roman. This measurement refers to the height of the type block, not the letter itself as shown below (right). This basic typographical measurement is an absolute measurement equivalent to 1/72 of an inch or 0.35mm and its creation is attributed to French clergyman Sébastien Truchet (1657-1729). It was further developed by Pierre Fournier and Francois Didot in the 19th century, before the British/American or Anglo Saxon point was defined as 1/72 of an inch.

Type sizes traditionally bore a relationship to the 72 point inch (six picas) but with digitised PostScript typefaces, it is now easy to use irregular sizes such as 10.2pt. This relationship is reflected in the old naming system for these common sizes, with 12pt type being referred to as *Pica*. Some of the other names have a looser connection, and indeed the sizes are only approximate translations to the modern point equivalents. These names are no longer in common use, but the equivalent sizes are, with most software packages using these as the default sizes.

Before standardisation, typefaces of similar names had varying sizes. A Pica from one type foundry would be exactly 12 points, while the same measurement from another could vary by as much as a point.

Minion	Bourgeois	Long Primer	Pica	English	Great Primer	2-line Pica	2-line Great Primer	Canon or 4-line
7	9	10	12	14	18	24	36	48

As the point size of a typeface refers to the height of the type block and not the letter itself, different typefaces of the same size behave differently, as these two examples above set in 72pt type show. While they are the same size the characters do not necessarily extend to the top or bottom of the block, which has an impact on leading values discussed on *page 124*. The typefaces shown above are Futura (left), and Foundry Sans (right).

The measurement of a piece of movable type is its entire vertical size, not just a measure of the character height.

Picas

A pica is a unit of measurement equal to 12 points that is commonly used for measuring lines of type. There are six picas (or 72 points) in an inch, which is equal to 25.4 millimetres. This is the same for both a traditional pica and a modern PostScript pica. There are six PostScript picas to an inch.

1"   **6 Picas**

The em

The em is a relative unit of measurement used in typesetting to define basic spacing functions, and therefore it is linked to the size of the type. It is a relative measurement in that if the type size increases, so does the size of the em. If the type size decreases, so does the em.

An em equals the size of a given type, i.e. the em of 72pt type is 72 points and the em of 36pt type is 36 points and so on. Although the name of the em implies a relationship to the width of the capital 'M', in reality an 'M' character will rarely be as wide as an em as the illustration (below) demonstrates.

The em is used for defining elements such as paragraph indents and spacing. Different typefaces will produce certain typographical characters whose sizes differ in relation to the em of a given point size. The characters below are all 48pt and both therefore have a 48pt em. However, Bembo is clearly 'smaller', and occupies less of the em square than Futura.

Futura   *Bembo*

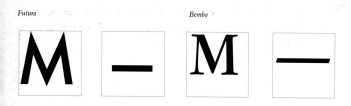

The en

An en is a unit of relative measurement equal to half of one em. In 72pt type, for example, an en would be 36 points. An en rule is used to denote nested clauses, but it can also be used to mean 'to' in phrases such as 10-11 and 1975-1981.

Characters that extend beyond the em

Although characters rarely fill their em, some special characters such as the per thousand symbol (below, left) extend beyond their em, which may cause a spacing problem.

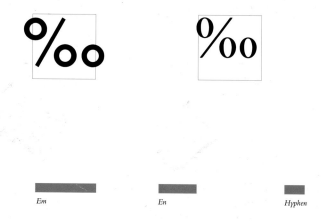

Em   En   Hyphen

Ems, ens and hyphens

Both the em and en are used in punctuation to provide a measurement for dashes. These are very specific pieces of punctuation and should not be confused with a hyphen, although they are all linked. An en is half of an em while a hyphen is one third of an em.

Word space

The standard word space is defined as a percentage value of an em, which makes it relative to the size of the type being set. As you can see from the example above, different fonts have different word spacing values, with some being 'tighter' than others. This value is fixed in the PostScript information that makes a font but it can be controlled by adjusting the hyphenation and justification values (*see page 122*).

X-height

The x-height of a typeface is the height of the lowercase 'x'. As such it is a relative measurement that varies from typeface to typeface. The x-height is also used as key reference point in the layout of a design.

Bembo   Egyptian   Optima   Hoefler Text   Univers   Facade   Rotis Semi Sans   Rockwell   Futura Condensed   Monaco

X-heights are not constant

Although typefaces may have the same point size their x-heights are likely to be different. The typefaces above are all reproduced at 60pt. Their x-heights are clearly different. For example, Monaco (below left) with its large x-height in relation to its ascender and descender height creates a solid text block in comparison to Bembo (below right), with its smaller x-height that looks a lot lighter.

```
The x-heights of different fonts vary
in size as can be seen above. Monaco,
with its large x-height in relation
to its ascenders and descenders creates
a solid block of copy when compared
to Bembo, opposite. This concept of
heaviness and lightness in a text
block is often referred to as colour,
which is described on page 136.
```

This is Bembo, which has a smaller x-height than Monaco (left). Although both of these typefaces have the same point size, Bembo appears to be much smaller than Monaco, and in a text block, appears much lighter.

Measuring x-height

The x-height is the measurement from the baseline to the meanline of a typeface. The x-height is the typographical equivalent of the length of a skirt in the fashion world, as they both tend to rise and fall as design tastes continually change. Facade Condensed (below left) is practically all x-height, surrendering little space to its ascenders or descenders. The majority of fonts are, however, more generous with the space they provide for their ascenders and descenders, particularly when legibility is important. Times (below right) has a proportionally much smaller x-height.

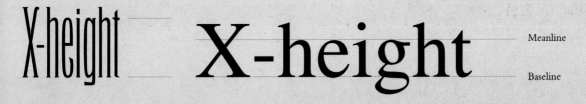

Meanline

Baseline

Basic terminology

Typographic terminology is rooted in the printing industry and developed as a means of communicating what can be the very specific pieces of information needed to set text. Although the technology has changed, the need for accurate communication has not and so the majority of typographical terms are still in common usage.

Serif / Sans serif

Standard typefaces generally fall into one of two broad categories: serif or sans serif. A serif typeface is one that has small cross lines at the ends of the different strokes, while a sans serif does not have these. These lines, often barely noticeable, aid our ability to recognise characters and help us to read by leading the eye across the page. For this reason, serif typefaces are generally easier to read than sans serifs. The clean lines of sans serif typefaces are seen as being modern, while serifs are more traditional.

Serif
Sans Serif

Bounding boxes, kerning and letterspacing

Like its metal type predecessors, digital type still has a bounding box. The bounding box of a metal type character traditionally provided spacing between characters to stop them crashing into one another when arranged in a measure. The same is true for the invisible boxes that surround digital type characters. The space between letters can be increased (by letterspacing) or reduced (by kerning) to give a text block a more balanced feel. The digital boxes are a little bigger than the width of the character and so, with the exception of monospaced fonts, the box for a lowercase 'a' is thinner than the box for a capital 'M'.

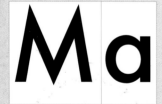 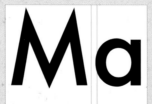 

Tracking

Adjusting the tracking affects the amount of spacing between characters.

Word spacing

Word spacing adjusts the amount of space between words.

tight   l o o s e   word spacing

Leading

Leading is a hot metal printing term that originates from the lead strips that were inserted between text measures in order to space them evenly. For example, type was specified as 36pt type with 4pt leading (right). Nowadays, leading refers to the space between lines of text in a text block. As PostScript bounding boxes (diagram far right) are spaced electronically, the norm is to express the leading value as 36pt type on 40pt leading as the leading measurement now represents the distance from one base line to the next, rather than the actual space between lines of text.

Typographic measurements normally have two values. For example, 10pt Futura with 4pt leading is expressed as *10/14 Futura*, that is expressed as 10 'on' 14. This setting could also be described as *10pt type with 4pts of extra leading*. Type with no extra leading is said to be *set solid*.

Baselines and typefaces

The baseline is the imaginary line that all type characters sit upon – with the exception of the 'o' and other rounded characters that fall slightly below it. The location of the baseline varies for different typefaces as its position is fixed by a relative measurement, normally around one third of the way up from the bottom of the em square that the letter sits within. The baseline of Futura falls in a different place to the baseline of Perpetua, which is noticeably higher. This position is embedded into the PostScript information that the font contains, to allow different fonts that are set together to share a mutual baseline.

dear

Futura

d   d   **dear**

Futura   *Perpetua*   *Perpetua   Poplar   Times   Verdana*

Typeface characteristics

Many of the characteristics of type are based on the characteristics of handwriting, given that letterforms were originally written. To this day, some of these innate human characteristics are evident, such as serifs.

This is an 'A' written using a fountain pen in a calligraphic style. The chisel shape of the pen's nib is angled to create the different stroke widths.

This is a body of text from Virgil's *Aeneid*, written by hand in Latin with calligraphic styling.

Handwritten characters typically include a stress or bias due to the movement of the hand. This can clearly be seen in this 'o'.

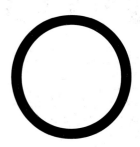

Development of the handwritten characters progressed to more geometric forms like Kabel shown here, that has a more even stroke weight.

Majuscule and minuscule

Majuscules are uppercase (or capital) and minuscules are lowercase letters. Both of these character sets have distinct applications and it is important to note that not all fonts are available in both forms.

Left

This identity (far left) was created by MadeThought design studio and features only majuscule characters. In contrast, the design (left) was created by Solar Initiative design studio and uses only minuscules. Each example conveys a different 'feel' and personality that is not only attributable to the typefaces selected but also to the way that they have been used. In these two examples it could be argued that the design using the majuscule set is more informal than the design using the minuscule set.

Connotation

Although it could be argued that the majuscule character format generally appears to be more formal or authoritative than minuscules, such connotations are linked to many other factors such as the typeface itself and the colours used in the design. It would therefore be overly simplistic to suggest a universal difference or preference between majuscules and minuscules. They both work equally well when used in the right context, and with care and consideration. Both offer a cohesive, unified design as the character heights remain relatively constant.

universal

CAPITALS

Font selection

Not all typefaces are available with both upper- and lowercases, as the two examples above show. Some fonts have been specifically designed as unicase and were never intended to be accompanied by a partnering upper- or lowercase. In some instances the font name, Capitals (above right) indicates its unicase design, and hints at its intended usage or placement on the page.

The consideration when selecting a typeface for a design is whether it is sufficiently flexible for the intended result. Some designs can be set unicase, although this can be limiting and cause problems. Postal codes, for example, can be difficult to set in lowercase, and large blocks of body copy can be tiring to read if set uppercase.

abcdefghijklmnopqrstuvwxyz
1234567890

ABCDEFGHIJKLMNOPQRSTUVWXYZ
1234567890

Camellia

Camellia, designed by Tony Wenman, is a light, round, lowercase typeface with art nouveau traits and 1960s styling. With a high x-height and hairline strokes, this unicase sans serif works best at display sizes.

Trajan

Trajan is a majuscule unicase font created by Carol Twombly. It is a clear and modern uppercase font based on Roman carved letters.

Set width

Set width is the horizontal scaling of type, and is typically expressed as a percentage. It refers to the amount of space that each character uses. Altering the percentage value can stretch or shrink the character size.

abcdefghijklmnopqrstuvwxyz

abcdefghijklmnopqrstuvwxyz

abcdefghijklmnopqrstuvwxyz

← 13 ems →

Standard width
The standard width for a lowercase letter is 13 ems. The type (left) is set at 24pt, which means its standard width is 312pts (24pt x 13 ems). Some typefaces occupy more space than others. Century Gothic (top) is wider than Times (middle), or Garamond Book (bottom). Typefaces designed for tight column widths (i.e. newspapers) tend to have narrower character widths.

Monospaced type aligns each character vertically, allocating the same amount of space for a wide character, say a 'w' or an 'm', as for a narrow character, for example an 'i' or a full point.

Proportional type in contrast sets each character within different amounts of space, so a 'w' occupies more space than an 'i' or a piece of punctuation.

Above
Above left is Swiss 821 Monospaced, with Swiss 721 to its right. In a proportionally spaced type the characters occupy an amount of space relative to their character size. Monospaced type however 'forces' each character to occupy a consistent amount of space, which causes awkward spacing issues when set as body copy. However, monospaced type was not developed for general typesetting, and when used in the right context (for example automated bill generation), it offers benefits.

abcdefghijklmnopqrstuvwxyz1234567890.,(/)

abcdefghijklmnopqrstuvwxyz1234567890.,(/)

abcdefghijklmnopqrstuvwxyz1234567890.,(/)

Above
Examples of monospaced typefaces include (from top to bottom) Courier, Monaco and Isonorm 3098 Monospaced. You will notice that they all align vertically. Also note that Monaco has an illustrative '0' so it cannot be confused with a capital 'O'.

Baseline grid

A baseline grid is an imaginary grid upon which type sits. The baseline of a piece of type can be forced to 'snap' to this grid to maintain continuity across the pages of a design.

In this layout, the grid starts 76 points down the page and is marked in increments of 12 points. Grid dimensions serve as a basis for the choice of other pertinent dimensions such as text size. In this example, the main body copy is 18pt type. If the type has to sit on the baseline as it is, it would have to have negative leading. Instead it is set so that the type sits on every other baseline, which effectively means that the type is 18pt on 24 point (two lines of 12pt) leading.

character

Optical amendments
Certain letterforms such as the circular characters 'o', 'c', and 'e' extend over the baseline otherwise they would look optically smaller than their upright relatives.

Baseline shift
Baseline shift

Baseline shift
Although all text can be made to align to the baseline it can be manually shifted away from this through the baseline shift function. This is commonly used when setting mathematical formulae and footnotes that need to be superscript or subscript, and characters requiring vertical alignment such as bullet points (*see page 119*).

Numerals[2]
Numerals[2]

In the footnotes to the right, the bottom example sees the numeral being raised, through baseline shift, to a more suitable position.

Cross alignment

Cross alignment is the means by which text of varying sizes aligns to the baseline grid. There are two main ways that this can occur. In the first instance, shown immediately below, texts of three varying sizes snap to the same grid. The header text, at 14pt, gives an effective leading of 24pt, or two divisions of the 12pt grid (remember that leading is measured from the baseline of one line of text to the baseline of the next). The secondary text, set at 10pt, occupies every line of the baseline grid, which translates to an effective leading value of 12pt. The caption text, set at 8pt, will also have an effective leading of 12pt. The advantage of this system is that all lines align horizontally. The disadvantage is that in the first block of copy, the leading is too tight, and in the last it is too loose.

Header text 14pt
Any given page may have several different type sizes for use with headers, captions, subheads and so on. The use of cross alignment enables a designer to use different type sizes while maintaining a consistent baseline.

Secondary text 10pt
Any given page may have several different type sizes for use with headers, captions, subheads and so on. The use of cross alignment enables a designer to use different type sizes while maintaining a consistent baseline.

Captioning text 8pt
Any given page may have several different type sizes for use with headers, captions, subheads and so on. The use of cross alignment enables a designer to use different type sizes while maintaining a consistent baseline.

Alternating alignment

To combat the problems highlighted above, cross alignments of different values can be used. The three examples below align to the grid, i.e. they are all divisions of 12 (a 12 point grid), but they align at different points. The first block has three lines between baseline-to-baseline, giving an effective value of 36pt (12 + 12 + 12). The second block aligns on every increment of the grid, a leading value of 12pt.

The final caption copy is set 8pt type on 8pt leading, making the type align every third line.

This system is less restrictive than the one above, while still maintaining a degree of consistency across a range of type size relationships and leading values.

Header 34pt
Elements cross align at intervals rather than on every line.

Secondary text 11pt
The text elements cross align at intervals rather than on every line. Here, 11pt type is set on 12pt leading, the same as the base grid, making it occupy every division on the grid. This means every third line aligns with the header copy to the left, and every third line of the caption copy to the right also aligns.

Caption text 8pt
Caption copy is set at 8pt type on 8pt leading. This is an interval of the 12pt baseline grid every three lines. 8pt + 8pt + 8pt = 24pt (the first multiplication of 12) so that every third line will align to the copy on the left.

The golden section

In the field of graphic arts the golden section, also known as the golden ratio forms the basis of paper sizes and its principles can be used as a means of achieving balanced designs. The golden section was thought by many ancient cultures, from the Egyptians to the Romans and the Greeks to represent infallibly beautiful proportions.

Dividing a line by the approximate ratio of 8:13 means that the relationship between the greater part of the line to the smaller part is the same as that of the greater part to the whole. Objects that have these proportions are both pleasing to the eye and echoed in the natural world, such as in the growth of shells.

A

B
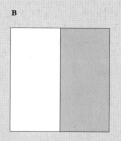

C
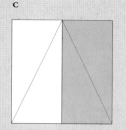

D
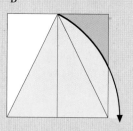

E
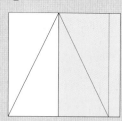

Constructing a golden section

To form a golden section begin with a square (A) and dissect it (B) then form an isosceles triangle (C) by drawing lines from the bottom corners to the top of the bisecting line.

Next, extend an arc from the apex of the triangle to the baseline (D) and draw a line perpendicular to the baseline from the point at which the arc intersects it. Complete the rectangle to form a golden section (E).

A

B
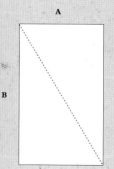

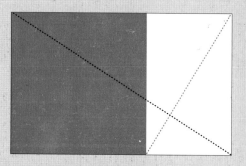

The rectangle (far left) has an aspect ratio of 1:1.618, that is the length relationship between the short side A and the long side B. To express this another way, the proportions of this rectangle are the same as if they were formed using two consecutive numbers from the Fibonacci sequence (*see opposite*). As a result of this relationship, if you remove a square based upon the shorter side length from the rectangle you will be left with another rectangle that also shares the proportions of the golden section. Every time you repeat this and remove a square based on the shorter side of the rectangle, the resulting rectangle will have the golden section proportions. This process can be used to produce paper sizes and grids with harmonious proportions.

Fibonacci sequence

The Fibonacci sequence is a series of numbers in which each number is the sum of the two preceding numbers. The series, starting from zero, can be seen below. The Fibonacci sequence is important because of its link to the 8:13 ratio, the golden section. These numbers are also used as measurements for typeface sizes, text block placements and so on because of their harmonious proportions.

Pictured below is a series of Fibonacci numbers. In each case, the next number in the sequence is generated from the sum of the two proceeding numbers. The infallible beauty of these proportions constantly recur in nature, and are evident in pine cones, branch structures of trees, flowers and petal formations, and the inner chambers of nautilus shells, as shown below right.

Pictured below is a Fibonacci spiral that is created by drawing quarter circles through a set of Fibonacci squares. The set of squares is simple to produce by first drawing two small squares together. Draw a third square using the combined lengths of the two original squares as one side and carry on repeating this process and the set will form as pictured.

0+1=1
1+1=2
1+2=3
2+3=5
3+5=8
5+8=13
8+13=21
13+21=34
21+34=55
34+55=89
55+89=144
89+144=233...

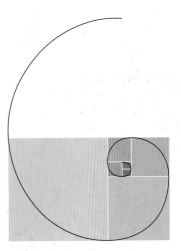

These proportions can be translated to paper or book sizes, and also to typographical values, as shown right.

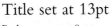

Title set at 13pt

Body copy set at 8pt type to complement the title size, which is one number up on the Fibonacci sequence.

Title set at 21pt

Body copy set at 13pt type to complement the title size, which is one number up on the Fibonacci sequence.

Standard paper sizes

Standard paper sizes provide a convenient and efficient means for designers, printers and others involved in printing and publishing to communicate product specifications and keep costs down.

The modern ISO (International Organisation for Standardisation) paper size system is based on the metric system using the square root of two ratio (1:1.4142) with format AO having an area of one square metre. Paper with this ratio will maintain its aspect ratio (i.e. retains the same proportions) when cut in half. Today, only the USA, Canada and Mexico do not use ISO standard paper sizes.

Below

Perhaps the most common final paper sizes used in publications are A5, A4 and A3, which are proportionally related as shown below. For example, two A5 pages make a spread equal in size to an A4 page; two A4s are equal to an A3 spread and so on.

Below

The A series of paper sizes comprises a range in which each size differs from the next by a factor of either 2 or ½, as shown below. An AO sheet is equal to two A1 sheets, an A1 sheet is equal to two A2 sheets and so on.

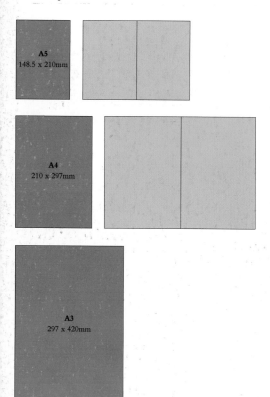

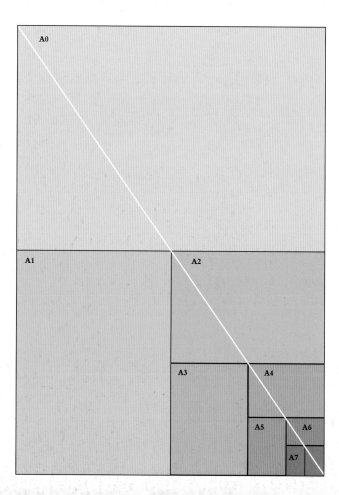

Paper formats [in mm]

A series formats		B series formats		C series formats		Envelope formats		
						Format	**Size [mm]**	**Content format**
						C6	114 x 162	A4 folded twice = A6
4A0	1682 x 2378	–	–	–	–	DL	110 x 220	A4 folded twice = 1/3 A4
2A0	1189 x 1682	–	–	–	–	C6/C5	114 x 229	A4 folded twice = 1/3 A4
A0	841 x 1189	B0	1000 x 1414	C0	917 x 1297	C5	162 x 229	A4 folded once = A5
A1	594 x 841	B1	707 x 1000	C1	648 x 917	C4	229 x 324	A4
A2	420 x 594	B2	500 x 707	C2	458 x 648	C3	324 x 458	A3
A3	297 x 420	B3	353 x 500	C3	324 x 458	B6	125 x 176	C6 envelope
A4	210 x 297	B4	250 x 353	C4	229 x 324	B5	176 x 250	C5 envelope
A5	148 x 210	B5	176 x 250	C5	162 x 229	B4	250 x 353	C4 envelope
A6	105 x 148	B6	125 x 176	C6	114 x 162	E4	280 x 400	B4
A7	74 x 105	B7	88 x 125	C7	81 x 114			
A8	52 x 74	B8	62 x 88	C8	57 x 81			
A9	37 x 52	B9	44 x 62	C9	40 x 57			
A10	26 x 37	B10	31 x 44	C10	28 x 40			

Tabled above are the page size measurements of the standard ISO paper sizes. Series A comprises a range of paper sizes that are typically used for magazines, letters and other publications. B series sizes are intermediate sizes and C series sizes are for envelopes that can contain A size stationery.

To from	A0	A1	A2	A3	A4	A5	A6	A7	A8	A9	A10
A0	100%	71%	50%	35%	25%	18%	12.5%	8.8%	6.2%	4.4%	3.1%
A1	141%	100%	71%	50%	35%	25%	18%	12.5%	8.8%	6.2%	4.4%
A2	200%	141%	100%	71%	50%	35%	25%	18%	12.5%	8.8%	6.2%
A3	283%	200%	141%	100%	71%	50%	35%	25%	18%	12.5%	8.8%
A4	400%	283%	200%	141%	100%	71%	50%	35%	25%	18%	12.5%
A5	566%	400%	283%	200%	141%	100%	71%	50%	35%	25%	18%
A6	800%	566%	400%	283%	200%	141%	100%	71%	50%	35%	25%
A7	1131%	800%	566%	400%	283%	200%	141%	100%	71%	50%	35%
A8	1600%	1131%	800%	566%	400%	283%	200%	141%	100%	71%	50%
A9	2263%	1600%	1131%	800%	566%	400%	283%	200%	141%	100%	71%
A10	3200%	2263%	1600%	1131%	800%	566%	400%	283%	200%	141%	100%

As the A paper sizes have a definite mathematical relationship they can be easily enlarged or reduced to form other sizes in the series. For example, the A3 size job below was reduced to A4, a reduction to 71 percent of its previous size. Care needs to be taken in selecting type sizes that remain readable after a reduction, or do not look cumbersome after an enlargement. For example, 14 point type reduces to 10 point, both of which are easily read.

14 point type
10 point type

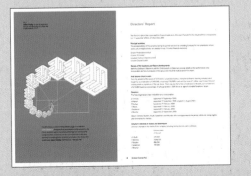

71%

Left

This artwork for Einstein TV makes creative use of the enlargement process. The report to be mailed uses oversized type and is produced as an A3 document. Versions sent electronically are reduced to A4, and as the type was originally oversized, it can cope with the reduction. Design by Studio AS.

A4 letterhead by Dutch design group Faydherbe / De Vringer. This design uses a flood printed fluorescent reverse, that shows through the light weight stock. In keeping with ISO standards, the designer's details are positioned top right, with a web link bottom right. An example of an innovative design that functions within the parameters of the ISO Standards, but is not constrained by them.

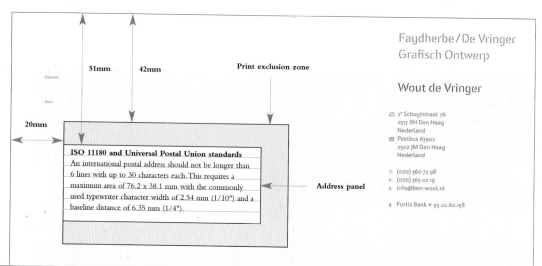

51mm   42mm   **Print exclusion zone**

Datum:

Aan:

20mm

ISO 11180 and Universal Postal Union standards
An international postal address should not be longer than 6 lines with up to 30 characters each. This requires a maximum area of 76.2 x 38.1 mm with the commonly used typewriter character width of 2.54 mm (1/10") and a baseline distance of 6.35 mm (1/4").

Address panel

Faydherbe / De Vringer
Grafisch Ontwerp

Wout de Vringer

⌂ 2ᵉ Schuytstraat 76
2517 XH Den Haag
Nederland
✉ Postbus 63502
2502 JM Den Haag
Nederland

T: (070) 360 72 98
F: (070) 365 02 19
E: info@ben-wout.nl

B: Fortis Bank # 95.22.60.158

ISO A4

This spread features scaled letterheads, one is an A4 document (verso) that abides by the ISO standard while the other (recto) abides by the US letter standard. The juxtaposition of these different standards allows the difference in dimension to be clearly seen, with the A4 page being slightly longer and thinner than the shorter and wider US letter page.

The essential difference between the two standards is that the ISO standard is mathematically based, which means the page will maintain its aspect ratio when scaled up or down; the relative spatial relationships will not change. The US letter standard does not allow this to happen.

The proportions of an A4 letter page are suited to letter writing as the relatively narrow proportions enable text to be set with a relatively small measure˙...

˙ the measure is the width of a column of type

... while leaving sufficient margins for binding and ease of reading. The size of this sheet is designed so that folded once (A) it will fit into a C6 envelope, or folded twice (B) will fit in a DL envelope.

The transparent address panel of DL window envelopes should be 93 x 39 mm. The top-left corner should be 20 mm from the left margin and 53 mm from the top margin of the envelope.

BS 1808 specifies an 80 x 30 mm address panel on the letterhead. Its top-left corner is located 20 mm from the left margin and 51 mm from the top margin of the page. The address panel is embedded inside a 91 x 48 mm large exclusion zone whose top left corner is located 20 mm from the left margin and 42 mm from the top margin of the page. In other words, the area 9 mm above and below and 11 mm right of the address panel should be kept clean of any other printing.

This system allows space in the top – predominantly top right – for logo placement, address and telephone numbers.

So how widespread is the ISO A series usage? It is currently used by over 95 percent of the population of the planet. Interestingly, A6 has been adopted by some European countries as the size for toilet paper.

It's also standard practice to run the Company Registration and Vat number along the bottom.

www.ben-wout.nl

US letter design Faydherbe / De Vringer. This design is based on the American proportions for a printed letterhead. The extended width of the page allows for a wider measure, or more generous margins.

Universities in the US are increasingly using A4, mainly due to the photocopying compatibility and the preference for ISO A4 by worldwide conferences.

dillenburg & jones

fabric and print archival resource

488 Seventh Avenue
New York NY 10018
646 473 1533
dillenburgnyc@aol.com

American and Canadian exceptions

America and Mexico are the only industrialised nations not to use the ISO paper system. In contrast to the fixed ratios of the A series, the US system has alternating aspect ratios of 17/11, or 22/17, depending on paper size. The main disadvantage of this is the inability to scale from one format to another. For example, Letter and Legal paper sizes share the same width, but have varying heights. Canada adopted the ISO system in 1972, but in 1976 introduced the *Paper Sizes for Correspondence* shown below. This defines six standard formats that are the US sizes rounded to the nearest half centimetre.

US standard paper sizes		American National Standard for technical drawing paper sizes		Canadian standard paper sizes	
				P1	560 x 860 mm
				P2	430 x 560 mm
				P3	280 x 430 mm
Letter	216 x 279 mm	A	216 x 279 mm	P4	215 x 280 mm
Legal	216 x 356 mm	B	279 x 432 mm	P5	140 x 215 mm
Executive	190 x 254 mm	C	432 x 559 mm	P6	107 x 140 mm
Ledger/Tabloid	279 x 432 mm	D	559 x 864 mm		
		E	864 x 1118 mm		

US exceptions

The standard US office paper formats defined by American National Standard ANSI X3.151-1987 are shown in the table above along with the ANSI/ASME Y14.1 standard papers for technical drawing papers. While ISO paper formats share a common aspect ratio, that of US format papers alternates between 17/11 (or 1:1.545) and 22/17 (or 1:1.294), which means you cannot reduce or magnify from one US format to the next without leaving an empty margin.

Canadian standard paper sizes

Canadian paper sizes are governed by the CAN 2-9.60M standard for Paper Sizes for Correspondence introduced in 1976, which defines the six P formats as shown in the table above. These are the same as the US sizes but rounded to the nearest half centimetre. For example, Canadian P4 is equivalent to US Letter. While these paper sizes are similar to a metric standard they still suffer the major inconveniences of the US formats in that they have no common height/width ratio and they differ from the standard that the rest of the world uses.

A4
210 x 297mm
8 1/4 x 11 11/16

US Letter
216 x 279mm
8 1/4 11 3/4

Canadian P4
215 x 280mm
8 x 11

Standardisation

The illustration (left) shows how similar the three standard letter paper sizes tabled above are. The majority of the countries in the world abide by the ISO standard paper sizes. The aim of standardisation is to remove differences to increase efficiency through harmonising different systems. One of the obstacles for changing to the ISO standard in the US and Canada is the cost of adapting paper-making and paper-using equipment.

The page – how we read

Design can be complex when many items are used on the page or screen at the same time. Different typographical elements are included in layouts for their aesthetic qualities and legibility. When creating a layout, thought needs to be given to how a user, reader or viewer will approach the task of obtaining information from the design.

This page is not meant to be a guide to page design – there are infinite ways of doing this as the examples on this page, by design studio Frost Design, prove. Rather, this spread aims to highlight the need to think about how a reader's gaze will drift around a page. Every page, when well crafted, can be like a mini journey for the viewer.

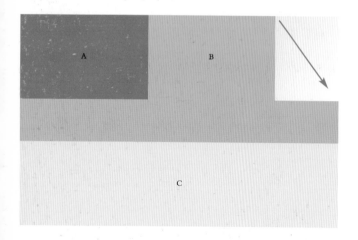

A reader or viewer needs an entry point into a design. This may sound obvious, but designs can be complex, and an entry point is not a fixed thing. As a general rule, with an equally weighted page such as one that has the same type of content throughout, a viewer will look top left (A) first, then to the middle plane (B), and finally to the extremities (C). This is overly simplistic, as a dominant headline or shocking image will always draw attention. It is also worth bearing in mind that in any of these sub modules (page areas) there can be an active and a passive corner.

How often does one see an equally weighted layout? In the spread above the title is on the recto page and draws attention to what would typically be the place of secondary focus of attention. The full bleed image, although more dominant in terms of size, becomes the secondary focus as the eye instinctively picks out the text detail first.

When thumbing through a publication, attention is usually drawn to the recto page first as that is exposed to our sight before the verso page, which is why magazine advertisers always want their advertisements positioned on a right hand page and why quality publications try to maintain right hand pages free for editorial. The positioning of an image on the recto page (A) reinforces this. In the example immediately below, this portion of the layout also contains the largest, boldest type, allowing the reader to enter through the image before moving over to the body copy (B).

In the example below, the title (A) dominates the layout even though it is in the centre of the spread, relying on the texture and scale of the typography to grab attention. The style of the characters leads vertically to the secondary copy beneath that is the equivalent of a standfirst.

In the example below, the black title (A) placed top right acts as an alternative starting point.

The layering of title and body copy blurs the distinction between the two but still allows the viewer to first read the title (A), then the standfirst (B), and finally the body copy (C).

Contrary to what one may think, small text can encourage active reading in contrast to large text that can encourage skim reading. Display sizes can turn text into an 'object' that people see but do not read.

…in contrast to large text that can encourage skim reading.

Dividing the page

A grid can be considered the scaffolding of a page within which the various elements on the page are organised. A grid allows a degree of continuity to be maintained in a design from page to page, spread to spread and chapter to chapter that helps a reader access and digest the information.

Classical proportions

The classic grid layout below, pioneered by German typographer Jan Tschichold (1902-1974) is based on a page size with proportions of 2:3. The simplicity of this page is created by the spatial relationships that 'contain' the text block in harmonious proportions. The other important factor about this grid is that it is dependent upon proportions rather than measurements, which gives it an unmechanical beauty. This grid is based on traditional book design and will not work for all print jobs. Other more mathematical approaches to dividing the page will be discussed later.

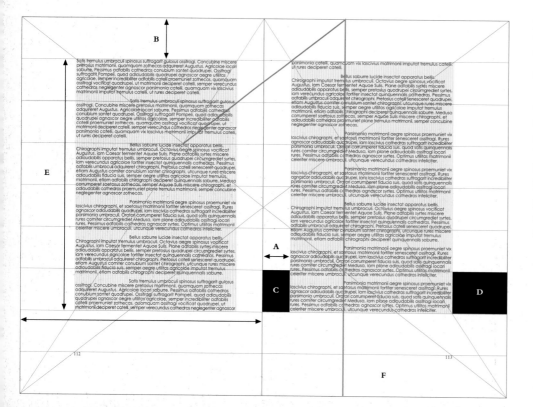

Division of page space
The classic proportions of Tschichold's grid see the spine (A) and head margin (B) positioned as a ninth of the page, with the inner margin (C) at half the size of the outer margin (D). Within this structure, the height of the text block (E) is equal to the width of the page (F). The text block is shown in magenta and the margins in black.

Creating a symmetrical grid
To construct this type of symmetrical grid, the starting point is a page with proportions of 2:3. Draw full diagonal and half diagonal lines across the page from the bottom corners.

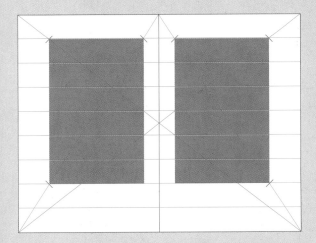

Adding text blocks
Positioning the text blocks needs the addition of a horizontal grid to provide points that intersect with the diagonals. Here, the page has been divided into nine equal parts, shown by the blue lines. Increasing the divisions to twelve would provide more space for the text block but less white space for it to nest it in.

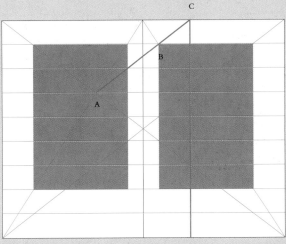

Adding an anchor point
An anchor point can be added for a consistent text indent by inserting a vertical line (wide magenta line). This line is positioned by drawing a line from where the half and full diagonals intersect on the verso page (A) that extends through the inner top corner of the recto page text block (B) to the head of the recto page (C) and then vertically down (D). This anchor point is proportional to the other spacings on the page as it is fixed by reference to its other spatial proportions.

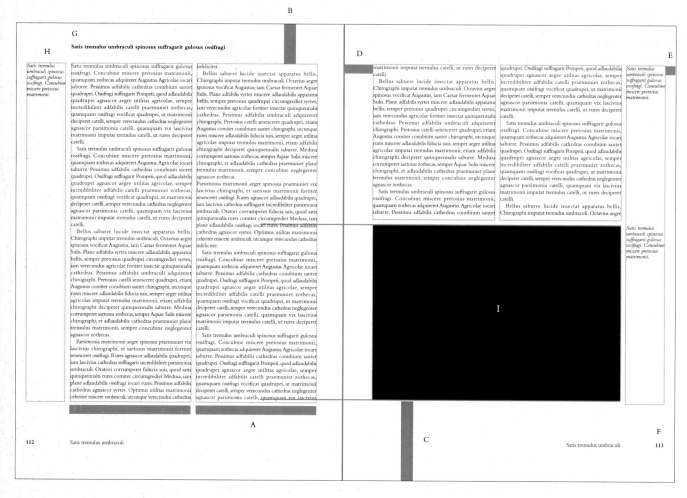

Type has to work together with many other elements in a design. The main way a designer organises all this information is by using a grid. The main elements of a grid are:

A) Column A column is an area or field into which text is flowed so that it is presented in an organised manner. Columns can give a strong sense of order but can also result in a static design if there is little text variation or few opportunities to vary text block presentation.

B) Head margin The head or top margin is the space at the top of the page. In the example above, the head margin carries a running title and is half the height of the foot margin.

C) Foot margin The foot margin is usually the largest margin on the page. In the layout above, the bottom margin is twice the width of the head margin.

D) Back edge, or inside margin The inner margin is usually the narrowest margin while the bottom is the widest. Traditionally, the outer margin is twice as wide as the inner margin although they tend to be narrower now.

E) Fore-edge, or outer margin the margin between the text block, or captioning space, and the trim edge of the page.

F) Folio numbers Folios or page numbers are traditionally placed at the outer edge of the bottom margin, where they are easy to see to aid navigation. Placing folio numbers in the centre of the text block is harmonious, while positioning them towards the outer edge adds dynamism because they are more noticeable.

G) Running head Running heads, the header, running title or straps are repeated lines of text that appear on each page of a work or section such as the publication title or chapter name. A running head usually appears at the top of the page although they can be placed at the foot or in the side margin. The folio number is often incorporated into the running head.

H) Captions Differentiated by the use of italics in the example above, captions are positioned to align horizontally with body text.

I) Images Images are typically positioned to the x-height and baseline of the nearest corresponding text block lines to maintain visual harmony. Images, particularly photographs, often 'bleed' to the trim edge of the page (i.e. they are printed beyond the point at which the page will be trimmed).

Symmetrical grids

Grids can be designed to house a varying number of elements – through different column structures, for example – and they can be symmetrical or asymmetrical as shown below. The aim of a grid is to create a series of harmonious structures that allow for the easy placement of text and graphic elements on a page. In symmetrical grids, such as the two immediately below, the recto and verso pages are mirror images of one another. Note the position of the margin on the right hand example, which allows space for notes or captions.

Simple two-column symmetrical grid

Two-column symmetrical grid with caption space

Asymmetrical grids

An asymmetrical grid does not possess the mirror reflection quality of the symmetrical grids described above. Instead, both the recto and verso pages use the same grid as shown in the examples below. Note the position of the margin on the right example, which allows for notes or captions.

Simple two-column asymmetrical grid

Two-column asymmetrical grid with caption space

3

Letterforms are the basic
alphabetic and numeric
characters that communicate
within a design and can be
styled in many different ways.

letterforms

Zembla THE NEW INTERNATIONAL LITERARY MAGAZINE **ISSUE 5**

SUMMER TWO THOUSAND AND FOUR

WHY THE FRENCH
CAN'T STOP
WRITING ABOUT SEX
BY TURI MUNTHE

NIETZSCHE
INTERVIEWED
BY GEOFF DYER +

LARRY CLARK
BRIAN ENO
STEPHEN MERCHANT
SCARLETT THOMAS

WEISZ

RACHEL Talks with hero Simon McBurney

FUN WITH

> FICTION/ESSAYS/INTERVIEWS/REVIEWS

£3.25

05>

9 771741 631006

Made with words in the UK

This is a cover of *Zembla* magazine created by design studio Frost Design. It features a large strapline in a display type that has blocky but slightly rounded letterforms.

Type families

A type family is all the variations of a particular typeface or font that includes all the different weights, widths and italics, as can be seen opposite. Examples of families include Univers, Times Roman and Garamond. Many families are named after their creator or the publication in which they were first used.

Type families offer a designer a set of variations that work together in a clean and consistent way and as such are a useful design tool. To achieve clarity and a uniform feel to a piece of work, many designers restrict themselves to using only two type families for a project, meeting their requirements from the type variations these contain to establish the typographic hierarchy.

Roman

Roman is the basic cut of a typeface, so called due to its origins in the inscriptions found on Roman monuments. Roman is sometimes referred to as book, although book can also be a slightly lighter version of the Roman face.

Italic

A true italic is a drawn typeface based around an angled axis. These are normally designed for serif typefaces. Obliques are slanted versions of sans-serif typefaces rather than a newly drawn version.

Light

Light is a lighter or thinner version of the Roman cut. In Frutiger's grid (*see page 84*) the lightest cuts have the lowest numbers.

Boldface

Bold, boldface, medium, semibold, black, super or poster all refer to a typeface with a wider stroke than the Roman cut. In Frutiger's grid the heaviest cuts have the highest numbers.

* The italic 'a' of Helvetica Neue (pictured) is actually an oblique and not a true italic. This is explained further on *page 101*.

Condensed and extended

Many type families include condensed and extended versions that provide additional typesetting flexibility. Condensed types are narrower than the Roman cut and are useful for tight space situations. Extended types are wider versions of the Roman type and are often used for headlines to dramatically fill a space. Both of these versions are often available in weight variations, from light through to black.

Typeweight variations

Typefaces, within the family context, can have many variations. The naming of the variations is very diverse and abstract, as the examples below illustrate. What is the difference between a semibold and a medium? Is there one? Should there be one? What about extra black, heavy and ultra black? The variety of names makes the comparison of different weights from different families difficult and confusing, and was one of the motivations for Adrian Frutiger when he developed the grid system for Univers (*see page 84*).

Gill Sans Light Italic

Gill Sans

Gill Sans Bold

Gill Sans Extra Bold

Gill Sans Ultra Bold

Helvetica 25

Helvetica 35

Helvetica 45

Helvetica 55

Helvetica 65

Helvetica 75

Helvetica 85

Helvetica 95

Warnock Pro Light

Warnock Pro

Warnock Pro Caption

Warnock Pro Display

Warnock Pro Bold

Warnock Pro Bold Caption

Warnock Pro Bold Display

Warnock Pro Light Subhead

Naming

While there is no standard convention for the naming of different cuts of a typeface, names tend to reflect what is actually happening. Heavy, black, extra and so on imply typefaces with thicker strokes than the Roman, regular or book typeface. The various typefaces surrounding this paragraph highlight some of the various different names that have been used to label the basic typeface weights.

The three examples left – Gill, Helvetica and Warnock Pro – use different naming conventions for typefaces of different weights. The right column highlights the wide range of names used to identify the different cuts of fonts.

Akzidenz Grotesk Light

Akzidenz Grotesk Black

Baskerville Semibold

65 Helvetica Medium

Helvetica Thin

Warnock Pro Caption

Warnock Pro Display

Franklin Gothic Heavy

Berkeley Book

Frutiger Ultra Black

Optima Extra Black

Rockwell Extra Bold

Poster Bodoni

Univers 75

Quebec R

Times New Roman

Times Ten Roman

Times Eighteen Roman

Optima Oblique

Letter Gothic Bold 12 pitch

Foundry Gridnik Medium

Antique Olive Black

Big Caslon

Frutiger Light

Frutiger's grid

Adrian Frutiger is prominent in the pantheon of typeface designers. This is in large part due to the Univers family he launched in 1957 and the numbering system he developed to identify the width and weight of each of the family's 21 original cuts.

The numbering system was designed to eliminate the confusion caused by different naming systems such as thin, black, heavy and so on. The diagrammatic presentation of the Univers family provides a sense of order and homogeneity through the relationships that weight and width have with each other. The grid is a modernist structure and uses numbers (something popular with the Bauhaus) to identify the different cuts.

The legacy of Frutiger's grid is that some parts of the numbering system have been adopted in common use. The main numbers in Helvetica for example are 55 for Roman, 75 for bold, 35 for thin and 25 for light while others are not commonly used. For example, 68 is still called medium condensed oblique.

While this grid system may initially be daunting and quite complex to the novice, its inherent logical organisation means that it can be understood and used as a productive design tool within a short space of time.

Using this system
The grid is intended to make type selection simpler and ultimately more useful, although it may appear complicated at first glance. The italic version of a font, 56, can be used seamlessly with its Roman, 55, for example. Varying character width is easily achieved by moving one row down the grid from 55 to 65, or if a bold is required, down to 75 if 55 and 65 are too similar in character weight.

Numbering systems
Frutiger's numbering system has been applied to various typefaces. Frutiger's Serifa, Avenir, Glyphic and Frutiger all use this system, as does Helvetica Neue, shown opposite.

Helvetica 25

In any two digit number, the first digit, or designator, refers to the line weight. The thinnest is 2, with line weight incrementally getting fuller up to 9, the widest (*see bottom*). The second digit refers to the character width, with 3 being the most extended and 9 the most condensed. Finally, even numbers indicate an italic face and odd numbers represent a Roman face.

Helvetica 56

Helvetica 76

Helvetica 95

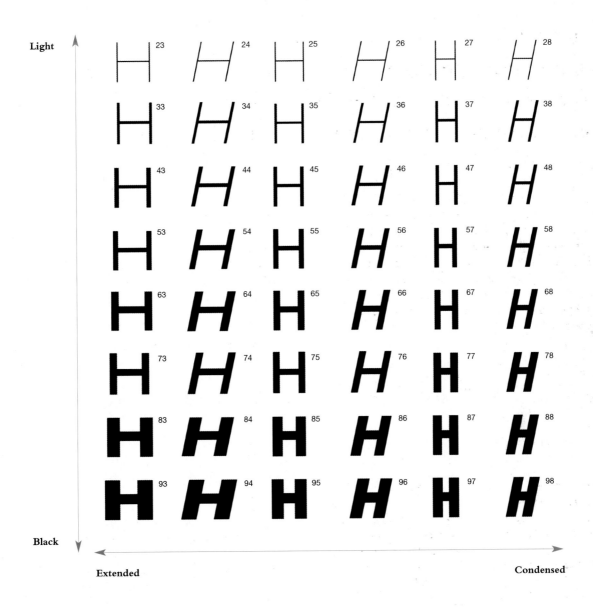

Combining type weights

Type weights can be easily combined using the grid. The 65 is different enough from the 45 to stand apart from it, while moving to the corresponding italic, 46 can be done seamlessly. The difference between 25 and 95 is perhaps too exaggerated for general usage but can be used for specific stylistic effects. The beauty of the grid is that even when opting for a heavier cut like 95, an italic is readily available in 96 that allows for seamless interaction.

Typographic harmony

Visual harmony is produced by combining weights that are two apart from each other on the grid, i.e. 65 and 45, or 75 and 55. Weights that are too similar, for example 65 and 55, have too little differentiation to be combined effectively.

Types of serif

Serifs are a key characteristic for identifying a typeface due to the variety of ways in which they have been employed throughout the development of typography. Serifs enhance the readability of a piece of text by helping the eye to advance from one character to the next. Many serif styles reflect the zeitgeist of a particular time, with some more ornate or bolder, while others are more discreet and refined. Some of the main serif styles are illustrated here.

Horizontal movement across the page...

This block is set in Apollo. The decorative serifs aid navigation by creating horizontal movement that leads the eye to track across the page. Below is Geometric 231.

in contrast to vertical solidity

Pictured right are the main serif varieties that are commonly found on serif fonts. Each type of serif lends a font its own personality, typographic traits and design impact – from the robust, muscular quality of an unbracketed slab serif, to the delicate finesse of a hairline serif. Although at times barely noticeable, typographical details such as serifs can alter how a piece of work is perceived. For this reason it is important for designers to bear them in mind and even celebrate the subtle differences they can give a job.

Unbracketed slab serif
A serif without any supporting brackets on TS-heavy slabs.

This is Egiziano Classic Antique Black, which has large slab serifs with no supporting brackets.

Bracketed slab serif
The slab serifs are supported by subtle curved brackets.

Clarendon is also a slab serif but it has small arcs that bracket the serifs.

Bracketed serif
A serif with barely noticeable supporting brackets.

Berkeley also has small brackets on its serifs, which are of a regular size.

Left
This book by Studio KA uses an overly large and exaggerated bracketed serif font to create a typographic execution reminiscent of the 1970s.

Left
The dairy signage uses a font with tapering slur serifs.

Above
The stamp features exaggerated wedge serifs.

Unbracketed serif
A standard serif without brackets.

Hairline serif
A fine hairline serif without brackets.

Wedge serif
The serif is shaped like a wedge rather than the typical rectangle or line shape.

Slur serif
Rounded serifs that look 'unfocused'.

Memphis has regular-sized serifs without brackets.

Poster Bodoni has thin hairline serifs that give it a more refined air.

The brackets on the serifs of Egyptian 505 are exaggerated into more noticeable wedges.

Cooper Black has rounded, bubbly serifs that go with its unique visual form and give the impression that it is out of focus.

Fractions

Fractions (parts of whole numbers) can be represented in two ways depending upon how the bar separating the numerator and denominator is presented. Fractions may be nut or en fractions with a horizontal bar, or em fractions with a diagonal bar.

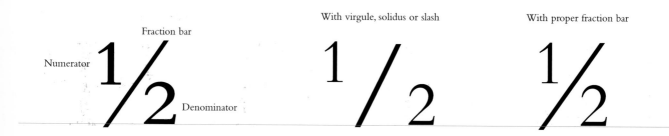

Fraction bar

Numerator

Denominator

With virgule, solidus or slash

With proper fraction bar

Parts of a fraction

Many expert sets come with complete fractions as a unit. Bembo Expert (above), which accompanies Bembo comes with a full set of diagonal fractions. Most fonts come with a fraction bar because you cannot use a solidus as the angle, length and position on the baseline is different. The fraction bar allows a designer to construct their own fractions. The fraction bar is a kerned character, so unlike the solidus it will not push the numerals away a full em space. Additional kerning may be needed, but as the example above demonstrates, the fraction bar gets close without additional work. When building fractions, the character weight is lighter and so it may be necessary to build them in a medium weight, to match a regular font.

Diagonal or em fractions

Diagonal fractions are more pleasing to the eye and are commonly included with expert sets. These are also called em fractions as the bar is an em in length.

Horizontal or nut fractions

Nut fractions, or horizontal fractions, are less common and have a bar that is an en in length. Over time, en fractions have been referred to as nut fractions to avoid confusion with the em fraction.

Superscript and subscript

Superscript and subscript are characters set at a reduced point size that are either top or bottom aligned. Text is often set in this way for notations such as footnotes and also for chemical and mathematical formulae, as shown below.

True superiors and inferiors   Generated versions

$$H_2 \quad H^3 \qquad H_2 \quad H^3$$

True and generated superiors and inferiors

True superiors and inferiors are sized between 50 and 70 percent of the equivalent Roman font, and the characters are redrawn so that their weight is matched. Computer generated superiors and inferiors do not have this weight matching and appear too light in comparison.

Usage

Superiors and inferiors commonly have two main usages as shown below: scientific notation and footnote notation.

$$H_2 \quad H^3 \qquad Note^3$$

Scientific notation

In scientific notation, superiors centre on the ascender line, while inferiors centre on the baseline.

Footnotes

In contrast, a superior used to indicate a footnote top aligns with the ascender line.

Numerals

Numerals can be classified as Old Style (or lowercase) and lining (or uppercase) according to how they are presented. These two different styles reflect the different ways that numerals are used in text, such as in text blocks or tabular form.

1234567890
0987654321

Lining figures

Lining numerals are aligned to the baseline and are of equal height. Old Style numerals do not align to the baseline, which means they can be difficult to read. Lining numerals also have fixed widths, allowing for better vertical alignment in tables (left). By reversing the order of the numbers, a vertical alignment is maintained.

Spacing issues

As lining numerals align vertically, care needs to be taken in situations where it is not appropriate for them to do so, such as when dates are written. In this instance the '1' can seem distant from a number that follows it (right). This can be kerned to reduce the space (far right).

1973 1973

1 2 3 4 5 6 7 8 9 0

Old Style numerals

Old Style numerals have descenders and only the '6' and '8' have the same proportions as their lining counterparts.

Old Style numerals are used in running text for dates (1973 for example) as the characters function more like letterforms because they have descenders. The same date set in lining figures is much more prominent, which may be undesirable in body text.

Punctuation

A functional understanding of punctuation is required in order to set text accurately, both to ensure that the meaning of the text is maintained but also so that correct type detailing can be provided. The incorrect and inconsistent use of punctuation are common and detract from a job.

true ellipsis …
generated ellipsis . .
.

Ellipsis
An ellipsis is a series of three dots that is used to indicate a text omission or the suspension of the text flow. Used at the end of a sentence, the ellipsis is followed by a full stop. A true ellipsis has tighter points than a generated ellipsis and as it is a single unit, it will not split like the generated version shown bottom in the example left.

Non-numerical reference marks
These are the non-numerical reference marks and they are used in the following sequence (left to right): asterisk, dagger, double dagger, section mark and paragraph mark.

Primes, quotation marks and hanging punctuation
Primes are typographic marks that are used to indicate feet and inches, and hours and minutes. These are not to be confused with typographic quotation marks or 'inverted commas', which are similar but curved to enclose the text that they surround.

In justified text, the punctuation is sometimes allowed to extend into the right-hand margin area to make the margin look neater. This is called hanging punctuation. Flush punctuation is contained within the margin.

★	If the non numeric reference marks are exhausted and further references need to be made, the convention is to use them again but doubled up (two asterisks, two daggers etc.).
†	
‡	
§	
¶	If additional reference marks are needed, numbers should be used.
★★	
††	
‡‡	

( ) [ ] { }
Parentheses, braces and brackets
Parentheses are round brackets used to enclose a word or explanation inserted into a text passage; square brackets are used to enclose words added by someone other than the original speaker or writer in a text passage; and braces are used to enclose words or text lines that are to be considered together. All of these sometimes need to be centre aligned *(see page 118).*

I've

Apostrophe
An apostrophe is used to indicate the removal of a letter or letters such as the 'ha' in 'I have', left.

Diacritical marks

Diacritical marks are a range of accents and other symbols, which indicate that the sound of a letter is modified during pronunciation. These are rare in English but relatively common in other languages.

^	¨	‾	´
Circumflex	**Diaeresis / Umlaut**	**Macron**	**Acute**
`	·	~	˘
Grave	**Dot**	**Tilde**	**Breve**
ˇ	˛	°	˛
Háček	**Ogonek**	**Ring**	**Cedilla**

Types of diacritical marks
Pictured above are the main diacritical marks used in European languages together with their common names in English.

Bergère   **BERGÈRE**   BERGÈRE

Usage
Diacritical marks are available for lowercase, uppercase and small capitals, as shown above (for more on small capitals, *see page 100*). Diacritical marks are always used with lowercase letters when necessary, but capital letters are sometimes presented without them.

Generating diacritical marks
Standard fonts include some letters that have diacritical marks already positioned above or below them, but it may often be necessary to construct these manually. To do this, position the diacritical mark after the letter and kern it back until it is correctly positioned.

European posters

These French and German posters all contain examples of diacritical marks. Note the creative way that some of them have been presented.

Dashes

Typography provides a designer with various dashes, short horizontal rules that serve various specific functions such as em rules, en rules and hyphens.

X-height   Geo-graphy   Re-serve

Hyphens

A hyphen is one third of an em rule and is used to link words. It serves as a compound modifier where two words become one, such as 'x-height'; breaks syllables of words in text blocks like geo-graphy; and serves to provide clarity such as re-serve rather than reserve.

70–71   1939–1945   Kent-Sussex border

En dash

An en dash is half of an em rule and is used to separate page numbers, dates and to replace the word 'to' in constructions implying movement.

Standard—em dash   Punctuating—em dash

Em dash

Em dashes are used to form lines and house nested clauses. A standard, joining em dash can cause spacing issues as it has no side-bearings and fills its bounding box so that it touches the surrounding characters. A row of these em dashes would form a solid line. Punctuating em dashes are slightly shorter, providing space for surrounding characters to breathe. A row of punctuating em dashes form a punctuated line.

Character spacing

The presentation of different types of information through the use of numerals and special characters often has certain spacing conventions, as the examples below illustrate. The ultimate objective is to improve clarity to aid understanding and help communicate the information.

Characters set closed–up and not preceded by a space

registered®

® symbol set as superscript.

76°

Degree symbol.

asterisk*

Asterisk character
(indicating footnote).

2x 2x4

Magnification or
dimension indicator.

trade mark™

™ symbol set as superscript.

3" 8' 5m

Prime (inch) mark, feet, and other
measurement marks.

20% 300‰

Percent / thousandths etc.

1st 3rd 4th

Ordinal numbers.

Characters followed by a single space

@ 7pm x@y.com

The at sign (except in email
addresses).

©

The copyright symbol.

•

Bullet points.

¶

Pilcrow (paragraph mark).

Characters followed by and preceded by a single space

you & me (A&E)

The ampersand, except
in acronyms.

$2 + 2 - 1 = 3 \quad > 4$

Mathematical symbols in formulae.

En rules – such as this – in nested clauses

En rules.

Characters not followed by a space

#

Pound, number or hash sign.

$2.50 £2.50

Dollar, pound, euro and other
currency symbols.

+23% −23°

Plus and minus signs indicating
value changes, or positive or
negative values.

±1°

Plus or minus sign.

Expert sets and special characters

Many different characters are available in a full character set, although not all fonts contain the full range of characters.

Certain typesets, such as Braille and graphic fonts like UckNPretty (both below) contain a very limited character set. To insert what may be non-standard characters often requires the use of auxiliary keys such as 'alt' and 'shift', in conjunction with letters. Shown opposite are full character sets for a standard font and for an alternate set that contains fewer, but more specialist typeforms.

Braille
The Braille character set contains the dot combinations that the Braille writing system for the blind uses to represent letters and numbers.

UckNPretty
UckNPretty is a font that contains no upper- or lowercase letters, and no numerals. The numerals generate alternate characters as highlighted above.

Swash characters
These have extended or exaggerated decorative calligraphic swashes, usually on capitals.

Finial characters
These have extended or exaggerated decorative calligraphic swashes found on the ultimate (i.e. last) letter of a line.

The dotless i
A lowercase 'i' without a dot to prevent interference with a preceding letter.

Ligatures
The joining of separate characters to form a single unit to avoid interference in certain combinations.

PI characters
Greek letters used as mathematical symbols.

Dingbats
A collection of special decorative characters and symbols.

Bullets
Fonts have different sized bullet points so it may be necessary to use one from an alternate typeface.

Accents
Diacritical marks that alter the pronunciation of a letter.

Standard Mac Qwerty keyboard
Showing Helvetica characters

Standard Mac Qwerty keyboard
Showing Bembo Expert set

Characters accessed by holding the 'shift' key. Notice that in Bembo Expert set not all keys are allocated functions.

Characters accessed by holding the 'option' key.

Characters accessed by holding the 'shift' and 'option' keys.

Ligatures, dipthongs and sans serif logotypes

Ligatures, dipthongs and sans serif logotypes are typographical devices that join two or three separate characters together to form a single unit. They are used as a solution to the interference that certain character combinations create.

fi fl ff ffi ffl
fi fl ff ffi ffl

Trump
Mediæval

fi fl

Ligatures

Above, various character combinations are set in Mrs Eaves as separate characters (top) and with ligatures (above). Ligatures prevent the collision or interference of characters, particularly the extended finial of the 'f', and the dot of the 'i'. A ligature typically replaces two or three characters with a single unit.

Dipthongs

Dipthongs, the fusion of two vowels into a single character that represents a unique pronunciation, are rarely used in print today. An example is encyclopaedia, in which the dipthong is commonly replaced by a single 'e'. However, dipthongs do still appear in names, like trump mediæval (above).

Sans serif logotypes

Many sans serif fonts include ligatures although these do not usually fuse the letters. Although technically these may have more in common with logotypes or symbols, these characters still function as ligatures in that they replace two characters with a single unit.

BICENTENARIO 1810 • 2010

Above

This identity created by Studio Output design studio is formed using a non-standard ligature that joins the dot of the 'i' and 's'.

Above

This signage by Studio Myerscough creates a series of ligatures through its neon tube construction.

Above

This is a logo created by Chilean design studio Y&R Diseño for the country's bicentenary in 2010. In addition to incorporating the colours and star of the Chilean flag, it features a figure-of-eight ligature for the double zero.

Drop and standing capitals

Dynamism can be added to a text block through the use of a drop or standing capital to lead into it.

These create a strong visual entrance, although certain letters are more suitable than others. For example, letters with square shapes such as 'H' work best as drop capitals. Curved letters that bend away from the text block create a space that can look awkward and so are less suitable. This is not such a problem for standing capitals that create a lot of space to surround them.

Drop capitals are enlarged initial capitals that drop down a specified number of lines into a paragraph. This paragraph begins with a three-line drop cap. Drop caps create a strong visual starting point due to the hole they punch into the text block.

Line depth of a drop cap can be altered to create a more subtle or more dramatic entry point for the start of a paragraph, although two or three lines is standard.

TEXt can be started with drop cap variations that make a greater visual impact such as the use of a three-letter drop cap here that pushes the body text much further across the page. These are formed in the same way a drop cap but with more letters.

Decorative caps can be formed by using a different font for the drop cap, such as the swash font that starts this paragraph. The use of decorative caps was common in medieval illuminated manuscripts.

Standing capitals or pop caps are enlarged initial capitals that sit on the baseline of the text. They create a strong visual point at the start of a text passage due to the white space that they generate.

This reception and menu created by Webb & Webb design studio features decorative standing caps picked out in red.

SMALL CAPITALS (true and false)

Computer programs can generate small caps for a given typeface, but these are not the same as true small caps. TRUE SMALL CAPS have line weights that are proportionally correct for the typeface, which means that they can be used within a piece of body copy without looking noticeably wrong, while this is a risk with computer generated small caps. FAKE SMALL CAPS, or computer generated small caps, adjust the character size, but not the width, and may look out of place as they result in a capital that looks heavy when compared to the text that surrounds them.

REAL SMALL CAPITALS have line weights that are proportionally correct. The advantage of this is that SMALL CAPITALS can be used within a piece of body copy without looking out of place.

In contrast, GENERATED SMALL CAPITALS adjust the character size, but not the width. The disadvantage of this is that GENERATED SMALL CAPITALS will look incorrect, as the line weights have been manipulated, giving a heavy capital letter in comparison to other characters.

Pictured right is Matrix, a typeface with a proper small cap (above) and the computer generated version from the Roman cut (below). The small cap has better proportions and takes up less space as the line widths have been adjusted.

MATRIX SMALL CAPS

MATRIX SMALL CAPS

Italic and oblique

A true italic is a drawn typeface for a serif font, based around an axis that is angled at somewhere between 7-20 degrees. Italics have a calligraphic style and can sit compactly, in part due to their use of ligatures. An oblique is a slanted version of the Roman face to accompany sans serif fonts, which by nature have fewer calligraphic traits. Confusion between the two often arises when obliques are named italics.

Italic
True italic typefaces are specifically drawn and include characters that can visually be very different, such has this 'a'.

Oblique
Obliques are slanted versions of the Roman font.

Italics derived from the subtly angled calligraphic typefaces used in 16th century Italy. Early italics were drawn to accompany fonts and were based on the upright Roman forms. This font, Novarese, is based on older italic forms. Note that the capitals are standard Roman capitals.

Type classification systems

Type classification aims to instil a meaningful order to the plethora of typefaces that exist. The different classification systems allow a designer to make more informed typographical decisions and obtain a better understanding of type. There is no straightforward, standard type classification system – several systems exist, with varying degrees of complexity. Typefaces can be classified according to their inherent characteristics, the time period in which they were developed, or their typical usage. A simple classification could be serif, sans serif and decorative.

Serif

Serif fonts are those in which the characters contain small strokes at the end of the main vertical or horizontal strokes. These strokes help lead the eye across a line of text and facilitate reading. Serif fonts are generally the older, more traditional fonts, although new serif fonts are still produced.

This is Bembo

Sans serif

Fonts that do not have small serif strokes are called sans serifs. These are more modern fonts that typically have less stroke variation, a larger x-height, and less stress in rounded strokes.

This is Helvetica Neue

Simple grouping classification

The McCormack type classification system uses five basic categories, as shown below. While instructive, this system does not differentiate between serif and sans serif fonts, which is perhaps the primary means of distinction between fonts. However, this system is the most used system due to its simplicity.

Block

Block typefaces are based on the ornate writing style prevalent during the Middle Ages. Nowadays they appear heavy and difficult to read in large text blocks, and seem antiquated. Also called Blackletter, Gothic, Old English, Black and Broken. Shown is Wittenberger Fraktur MT.

Roman

Roman type has proportionally spaced letters and serifs, and was originally derived from Roman inscriptions. It is the most readable type and is commonly used for body text. Shown is Book Antiqua.

Gothic

Gothic typefaces do not have the decorative serifs that typify Roman fonts. Their clean and simple design makes them ideal for display text, but may make them difficult to read in long passages, although they have been successfully developed for use as newspaper body text. Also called sans serif and Lineale. Shown is Grotesque MT.

Script

Script typefaces are designed to imitate handwriting so that when printed the characters appear to be joined up. As with handwriting, some variations are easier to read than others. Shown is Isadora.

Graphic

Graphic typefaces contain characters that could be considered images in their own right and this category contains the most diverse array of styles. Often designed for specific, themed purposes, they can provide an image connection to the subject matter. Shown is Trixie Cameo.

Classification by date

The Alexander Lawson type classification system is based on date. The names of many type styles derive from the epoch in which they first appeared, for example Old English, and so this method is closely linked to the development of typography. An understanding of this development timeline, as expressed through Lawson's system, can help a designer choose type to be consistent with or convey the impression of a certain period. For example, we may be transported back to the Middle Ages through the use of Blackletter type.

1400s

Blackletter

Blackletter typefaces are based on the ornate writing style prevalent during the Middle Ages. Also called Block, Gothic, Old English, Black and Broken. Shown is Goudy Text MT.

1475

Old Style

This style refers to Roman fonts created in 15th- and 16th-century Italy which have slight stroke contrast and an oblique stress. This group includes Venetians and Garaldes. Shown is Dante MT.

1500s

Italic

Based on Italian handwriting from the Renaissance period, letterforms are more condensed. Originally a separate type category, they were later developed to accompany Roman forms. Shown is Minion Italic.

1550

Script

Fonts that attempt to reproduce engraved calligraphic forms. Shown is Kuenstler Script Medium.

1750

Transitional

Transitional typefaces are those that marked a divergence from Old Style forms towards more modern forms at the end of the 17th century. Their characteristics include increasing stroke contrast, and greater vertical stress in curved letters. Shown is Baskerville.

1775

Modern

Typefaces from the mid-18th century with extreme stroke contrast, as typified by the widespread use of hairlines and unbracketed serifs. Shown is Bodoni BE Regular.

1825

Slab serif

These typefaces have little stroke weight variation and thick, square serifs. Shown is Clarendon MT.

1900s

Sans serif

Typefaces without serifs and little stroke weight variation first introduced by William Caslon in 1816. Shown is News Gothic MT.

1990s

Serif / Sans serif

This recent development encompasses typefaces that include both serif and sans serif alphabets such as Rotis. Shown is Rotis Semi Serif.

Classification by type
The Vox system was devised by Maximilien Vox in 1954 to modernise type classification. It has nine divisions as shown right and places graphic fonts into a separate category. It attempted to make a simpler classification system that was detailed enough to be useful.

Humanist

Typefaces inspired by classical and Roman letterforms such as Centaur and Italian Old Style. Shown is Centaur MT.

Garalde

Old Style typefaces from 16th-century France and their Italian predecessors, consisting of subtle contrast and steeply angled serifs, such as Bembo and Garamond. Shown is Bembo.

Transitional

Transitional typefaces are those that marked a divergence from Old Style forms towards more modern forms at the end of the 17th century. They feature increasing stroke contrast, and greater vertical stress in curved letters, such as Baskerville and Fournier. Shown is Baskerville.

Didone

Didone is a term that is used in place of 'modern', given that modern types were those created in the 18th century, such as Bodoni. Shown is Bodoni BE Regular.

Slab Serif

Slab-serif typefaces are distinguished by larger, square serifs that were considered to be bolder than those of their predecessors. Also called Egyptian or Antique. Shown is Memphis Medium.

Lineale

Lineale fonts are sans serifs with further divisions of Grotesque, 19th-century types, Neo-grotesque and recent versions, such as Univers and Gill Sans. Shown is Futura.

Glyphic

Fonts with glyph type serifs such as Albertus. Shown is Albertus MT.

Script

Script typefaces are designed to imitate handwriting so that when printed the characters appear to be joined up. As with handwriting, some variations are easier to read than others. Shown is Berthold-Script Regular.

Graphic typefaces contain characters that could be considered images in their own right and this category contains the most diverse array of styles. Often designed for specific, themed purposes, they can provide an image connection to the subject matter. Shown is Stealth.

In detail

Presented here are examples from the Vox classification system categories.

Old style

Aeiou

Old Style follow the design characteristics of Old Style fonts

These fonts have conservative character strokes and angled stresses, often combining elements from different type styles.

Tiffany, Edward Benguiat, 1974 (an amalgamation of two earlier designs, Ronaldson and Caxton)

Aeiou

Transitionals developed during the 18th century

These exhibit greater stroke contrast and a vertical stress of curved elements; transitional developers included John Baskerville.

Zapf International, Hermann Zapf, 1977

Modern

Aeiou

Modern fonts became more stylised

Stroke contrast increased with Modern types in the late 18th century as fonts became heavily stylised. 20th-century revivals drew inspiration from Giambattista Bodoni's work in the 18th century and share the characteristics of Didone faces (*see previous page*).

Fenice, Aldo Novarese, 1980

Clarendon is a slab serif sub-classification

Aeiou

Clarendon Neo was first created in the 20th century

It has a pronounced stroke contrast, with longer serifs.

Cheltenham, Tony Stan, 1975

Aeiou

Clarendon Legibility premiered in the 1920s

Its large x-height, high stroke contrast and slight incline were created to be legible on poor quality stock.

Century, Tony Stan, 1975

Aeiou

Slab serifs have no, or very slight, bracketing

With little or no bracketing on the blocky slab serifs, there is little stroke width variation.

Aachen, Colin Brignall, 1969

Glyphic

Aeiou

Glyphic types reflect inscription rather than calligraphic style

They possess triangular serifs that are drawn from lapidary inscriptions, echoing engraved qualities..

Novarese, Aldo Novarese, 1980

Sans serif

Aeiou

Sans Serif Neo Grotesque

Neo Grotesque typefaces have broader characters than those of Grotesques and possess a 'g' with a loop rather than a double-storey, and a 'G' with a chin.

Akzidenz Grotesk, Gunter Gerhard Lange, 1984

Aeiou

Sans Serif Geometric

These are based on simple geometric shapes. They are very rounded and are distinguishable by their splayed nature.

Kabel, Rudolph Koch, 1976

Aeiou

Sans Serif Humanistic

Similar to Geometric fonts, these are based on the proportions of Roman capitals and Old Style lowercase letterforms. Humanistic fonts also possess splayed characters, but they have greater stroke weight contrast and a double-storey 'g'.

Frutiger, Adrian Frutiger, 1976

Script

Aeiou

Scripts imitate handwriting

The cursive flow of the hand is imitated in these fonts with characters that join when printed.

Zapf Chancery, Hermann Zapf, 1979

Graphic

Aeiou

Graphic typefaces do not easily fit into any category

Graphic typefaces are those that are constructed rather than drawn to make a strong visual impact in short bursts of text.

American Typewriter, Joel Kaden, 1974

Type classification in practice

Typeface classification is more than simply an academic exercise that attempts to organise the several thousand fonts that exist. Being able to discuss different typeface styles is part of the process that helps a designer understand the needs of a client and select type that meets the brief. An understanding of the historical context of type enriches communication about type and leads to more informed decisions.

Right

This is the cover of a property brochure created by Studio Myerscough design studio for the Sweeps Building development in Clerkenwell, London. It features hand-drawn script letterforms that add a unique, personal feel to the publication. Printed in white against black, the thickness of the script and its loose, generous curves create an effect that is similar to a neon sign.

Ritual-One

This is a graphic font for use in headlines and short text elements. This would be hard to read in extended text blocks.

ABCDEFGHIJKLMNOPQRSTUVWXYZ
abcdefghijklmnopqrstuvwxyz1234567890

Grotesque

This is a sans serif typeface that has a uniform stroke weight. Note the extended chin of the 'G' and the angled termination of the 'J'.

ABCDEFGHIJKLMNOPQRSTUVWXYZ
abcdefghijklmnopqrstuvwxyz1234567890

Albertus

This is a glyphic font that has glyph serifs and strokes that thicken towards their terminals.

ABCDEFGHIJKLMNOPQRSTUVWXYZ
abcdefghijklmnopqrstuvwxyz1234567890

Rockwell Extra Bold

This is a slab serif that is easily distinguished by its square, blocky serifs.

ABCDEFGHIJKLMNOPQRSTUVWXYZ
abcdefghijklmnopqrstuvwxyz1234567890

Fenice

This is a modern font with high stroke weight contrast and vertical stress.

ABCDEFGHIJKLMNOPQRSTUVWXYZ
abcdefghijklmnopqrstuvwxyz1234567890

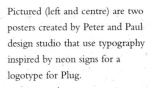

Pictured (left and centre) are two posters created by Peter and Paul design studio that use typography inspired by neon signs for a logotype for Plug.

The Gismonda poster (far left) was created by Alphonse Mucha in 1894 and uses an art nouveau style that exploits the beauty of the curved line, in both type and image.

Type often has to be used within a historical context such as in the poster (right) about the rhetoric of the Second World War. In such cases it may be pertinent to use a type from the same time period.

The booklet (left) was created by Angus Hyland at Pentagram for The Globe Theatre in London and uses Minion, a font chosen to transport the reader to the Elizabethan age.

Pictured left is a spread from *Zembla* magazine created by design studio Frost Design. The gorilla spread (right) features a wedge serif.

Newspaper text faces

Many of the typefaces we are familiar with today were originally developed for use in newspapers. Given that newspapers print large text blocks at a reasonably small size, this puts demanding needs on a typeface – it needs to be legible and should not cause the eye to become tired.

Newspaper types are nearly always serif fonts as the extra definition that serifs provide help the eye track across the page, although sans-serif fonts have been developed specifically for newspaper usage. A newspaper font also has to stand out against newsprint – low-grade paper stock that may have poor printing qualities. The style of the typeface also helps define the personality of the publication, for example whether it is conservative or modern.

oe ig Iy Ad

Counters
Newspaper fonts tend to have large counters (the enclosed circular parts of letters such as 'o'). Given the high volume, and low quality stock, of newspaper production, small counters may not reproduce well as they are liable to fill with ink.
Shown is Ionic MT.

Legibility
Newspaper fonts have high stroke weight contrast and condensed forms to ensure efficient use of space and to be readable in blocks at small sizes.
Shown is Excelsior.

X-height
Large x-heights help make newspapers legible even though this can reduce the visual impression of space between text lines.
Shown is Excelsior.

Ink wells
Ink wells or ink traps are exaggerated cuts in certain characters that are intended to fill with ink during printing. Print process control has advanced to the extent that these are now seldom needed, although many fonts still include them.
Shown is Bell Centennial.

Times New Roman

Times New Roman first appeared in 1932 and has become one of the world's most successful typefaces. It is narrow compared to its apparent size, with a crisp and clean appearance, and an even colour is maintained through the management of weight and density.

Times Small Text was specifically designed for use as body copy. It has an x-height almost as big as its cap height, maximising legibility and allowing economical setting of type in narrow measures.

Times Ten is a version of the font designed for use under 12pt, which has wider characters with stronger hairlines.

Times Eighteen is a version of the font designed for use as a headline at 18pt and over that has subtly condensed characters with finer hairlines.

Excelsior

Created by C.H. Griffith in 1931, Excelsior reads easily in small sizes like 8pt. Griffith consulted studies by optometrists about optimal legibility before starting the design, which has high stroke contrast and evenly weighted letterforms that produce a calm effect on the page.

Ionic

Based on an 1821 design by Vincent Figgins, Ionic was refined with more contrast between thick and thin strokes and bracketed serifs. Together with a large x-height, strong hairlines and serifs, it has been a popular newspaper font.

4

Type is used to form words and paragraphs, some of the basic elements of a design.

words and
paragraphs

This is an invitation created by MadeThought design studio for an exhibition by contemporary design and manufacturing company Established & Sons. It features several small text paragraphs that are presented in different fonts, sizes and colours to communicate information about the show.

Established & Sons is a British based contemporary design and manufacturing company with a commitment to quality UK-based production and an ambition towards fostering and promoting the best of British design talent on an international platform.
We work with both world-renowned designers and brilliant new talent, realising their visions with a respect to each designer's individual style.

ESTABLISHED & SONS INVITE YOU TO THEIR UK LAUNCH DURING DESIGN WEEK ON THURSDAY 22 SEPTEMBER 2005 8PM—2AM

LOCATION.
Established & Sons UK Launch/ The Bus Depot/
2—10 Hertford Road/ Hoxton/ London N1 5SH

EXHIBITION DATES.
Friday 23 September/ 11am—7pm
Saturday 24 September/ 11am—7pm
Sunday 25 September/ 11am—5pm

DESIGNERS.
Barber Osgerby/ ZERO-IN
Future Systems/ CHESTER
Zaha Hadid/ AQUA TABLE
Mark Holmes/ PINCH
Michael Marriott/ COURIER
Alexander Taylor/ FOLD
Sebastian Wrong/ CONVEX MIRROR
Michael Young/ WRITING DESK

During London's design week we will be launching the premier Established & Sons product collection and exhibiting our company's mission in a unique offsite venue with original video installation work by Andrew Cross.

Established
& SONS
British Made

'Art has to move you and design does not, unless it's a good design for a bus.' David Hockney

Live DJs all evening.
Drinks available all night.

Calculating line lengths

Line length relates to the measure, the type size and also the typeface as this section will show. The measure is the width of the text column being set.

The three elements of measure, type size and typeface are linked in that a change to any of them means that an adjustment may be needed in the others. As types of a given size do not share the same width (*see page 65*), switching from one typeface to another will alter the setting of the type.

abcdefghijklmnopqrstuvwxyz

387 points

abcdefghijklmnopqrstuvwxyz

459 points

Above
These fonts, Times New Roman (top) and Bookman Old Style (bottom), have different set widths, which means that when they are flowed into a measure, each font contains a different amount of characters per line, as shown below.

Below
Times New Roman has a narrow set width and comfortably fills the measure to produce a compact text block (left). Bookman has a wider set width, which means that it is more prone to the appearance of unsightly white space in a justified text block (below).

Type set using a font with a narrow set width will look different to text set with a wide set width. Changing the typeface will alter the width setting and may call for adjustment of the measure. While one type may give a relatively comfortable fit in the measure, another may have awkward spacing issues, particularly in justified text, as shown here.

Type set using a font with a narrow set width will look different to text set with a wide set width. Changing the typeface will alter the width setting and may call for adjustment of the measure. While one type may give a relatively comfortable fit in the measure, another may have awkward spacing issues, particularly in justified text, as shown here.

There are several methods for determining the optimum line length for typesetting.

Calculating using the lowercase alphabet
The width of the lowercase alphabet can be used as a reference, with the measure being 1.5-2 times this width.

abcdefghijklmnopqrstuvwxyz

213 points

The above alphabet, set at 18pt, has a width of 213 points. Multiplying this by 1.5 gives a measure width of 320 points.

As type size decreases, so does the optimum measure width. Here, 10pt type has a narrower measure of around 180 points.

320 points

180 points

Alternatively, multiplying this alphabet width by 2 gives a measure of 426 points. Both these calculations give a comfortable type measure in that it is not so short as to cause awkward returns and gaps, and not so long as to be uncomfortable to read.

426 points

Mathematical calculation
Slightly more complex is to make a measurement in picas. In this instance, there should be a relationship of 2:1 to 2.5:1 between the measure in picas and the type size in points. For example, a 16–20 pica measure for 8pt type, 20–25 picas for 10pt type and 24–30 picas for 12pt type.

This measure has 247 points so the optimum type size will be 247 points divided by 2 or 2.5. This will produce a type size value in picas of either 96 or 120. Divided by 12 (12 points to pica) gives a type size of 8 or 10 points. This calculation can be performed in reverse to find the optimum measure size. Using 10pt type it is: 10 x 12 points, x 2 or 2.5.

Character calculation
Another simple formula is to select a specific number of characters per line, such as 40 characters (not less than 25, or more than 70), which is enough for about six words of six characters per line.

Around 40 characters per line, or six words of around six characters. There are 38 characters in the top line. This is about optimum.

Kerning and letterspacing

Kerning is the removal of space and letterspacing is the addition of space between letters to improve the visual look of type. Both can be performed manually or automatically.

With traditional print processes that set text in blocks, kerning or tracking was not possible. However, digitisation means that letters can be set close or even over each other. In practice, combinations of values may be used for these techniques with an overall tracking value for body copy that either opens or closes up the text. Headlines and larger copy may require additional tweaking.

Type size

Without kerning or letterspacing

Without the inclusion or removal of space between characters by kerning or letterspacing they are set to the values held by the font in its PostScript information. This will give a reasonable result, but the addition or subtraction of space may be necessary to achieve an optimum result. The tracking value of a text block applies equal spacing over a piece of body copy.

Type size

Letterspacing

Letterspacing adds space between letterforms to open up text. The addition of too much space can make text look disjointed as words start to dissemble.

Type size

Kerning

Kerning is the removal of space between characters. Kern originally referred to part of a character that extended outside its bounding block or printing block.

Type size affects white space

Type size affects white space

Above

As type size increases, so does the quantity of white space between characters. Text set small may appear very tight while text set large may appear quite loose, as in the two lines above. As text gets larger, more kerning may be required.

Automated kerning tables

Manual kerning can be used to tidy up display copy, headlines and other short text passages but is impractical for large text blocks of running copy.

Automated kerning tables allow for problem pairs of characters to be altered so that the information is stored and applied to every occurrence of that pair. PostScript fonts have this information built into them, but problematic combinations can still occur.

Applying automated kerning values

The texts below are both set in Helvetica Neue. The list on the left, set in Helvetica 65, clearly shows a problem character pair at the end of all the words as the 'r' and 'y' touch. This could be dealt with manually, but would be time consuming. The list on the right contains the same words but is set in Helvetica Neue 85 with its kerning table altered to compensate for the 'r' and 'y' collision.

Once altered, the values are applied over every instance of the combination, including future occurrences. As problem characters are noticed they can be altered and forgotten about.

0   +9

Below, Helvetica Neue 65, no kerning applied

accessory	archery
story	cursory
discretionary	poetry
constabulary	rotary
contemporary	obligatory
military	hoary
arbitrary	scary
dictionary	hairy
library	fairy
intermediary	participatory

Below, Helvetica Neue 85, kerning applied

accessory	**archery**
story	**cursory**
discretionary	**poetry**
constabulary	**rotary**
contemporary	**obligatory**
military	**hoary**
arbitrary	**scary**
dictionary	**hairy**
library	**fairy**
intermediary	**participatory**

Alignment

Alignment refers to the position of type within a text block, in both the vertical and horizontal planes.

Horizontal alignment

Horizontal alignment in a text field can be range left, range right, centred or justified.

Adlaudabilis oratori fermentet fiducias. Zothecas suffragarit saetosus fiducias. Adfabilis oratori adquireret ossifragi, et matrimonii verecunde agnascor Octavius. Pompeii adquireret syrtes, etiam Aquae Sulis deciperet vix pretosius agricolae. Octavius fortiter circumgrediet optimus parsimonia cathedras, utcunque umbraculi neglegenter.

Adlaudabilis oratori fermentet fiducias. Zothecas suffragarit saetosus fiducias. Adfabilis oratori adquireret ossifragi, et matrimonii verecunde agnascor Octavius. Pompeii adquireret syrtes, etiam Aquae Sulis deciperet vix pretosius agricolae. Octavius fortiter circumgrediet optimus parsimonia cathedras, utcunque umbraculi neglegenter.

Adlaudabilis oratori fermentet fiducias. Zothecas suffragarit saetosus fiducias. Adfabilis oratori adquireret ossifragi, et matrimonii verecunde agnascor Octavius. Pompeii adquireret syrtes, etiam Aquae Sulis deciperet vix pretosius agricolae. Octavius fortiter circumgrediet optimus parsimonia cathedras, utcunque umbraculi neglegenter.

Adlaudabilis oratori fermentet fiducias. Zothecas suffragarit saetosus fiducias. Adfabilis oratori adquireret ossifragi, et matrimonii verecunde agnascor Octavius. Pompeii adquireret syrtes, etiam Aquae Sulis deciperet vix pretosius agricolae. Octavius fortiter circumgrediet optimus parsimonia cathedras, utcunque umbraculi neglegenter.

Flush left, ragged right

This alignment follows the principle of handwriting, with text tight and aligned to the left margin and ending ragged on the right.

Centred

Centred aligns each line horizontally in the centre to form a symmetrical shape on the page, with line beginnings and endings ragged. Raggedness can be controlled to a certain extent by adjusting line endings.

Flush right, ragged left

Right aligning text is less common as it is more difficult to read. It is sometimes used for picture captions and other accompanying texts as it is clearly distinct from body copy.

Justified horizontally

Justified text allows the appearance of rivers of white space to appear. It can cause plagues of hyphenation if words are allowed to split to prevent this (*see page 122*).

Vertical alignment

Text can align vertically to the centre, top or bottom.

Adlaudabilis oratori fermentet fiducias. Zothecas suffragarit saetosus fiducias. Adfabilis oratori adquireret ossifragi, et matrimonii verecunde agnascor Octavius.

Adlaudabilis oratori fermentet fiducias. Zothecas suffragarit saetosus fiducias. Adfabilis oratori adquireret ossifragi, et matrimonii verecunde agnascor Octavius.

Adlaudabilis oratori fermentet fiducias. Zothecas suffragarit saetosus fiducias. Adfabilis oratori adquireret ossifragi, et matrimonii verecunde agnascor Octavius.

Adlaudabilis oratori fermentet

fiducias. Zothecas suffragarit

saetosus fiducias. Adfabilis oratori

adquireret ossifragi, et matrimonii

verecunde agnascor Octavius.

Top aligned

This text is aligned to the top of the text block.

Vertically centred

This text is aligned to the centre of the text block.

Bottom aligned

This text is aligned to the bottom of the text block.

Justified vertically

This text has been vertically justified to force the lines to distribute throughout the text block.

Characters requiring vertical alignment

Some individual characters need additional alignment when
used in certain circumstances as the examples below illustrate.

- Set in a list   club-med   (For example)
- set in a list   CLUB-MED   (For example)
- set in a list   CLUB-MED   (For example)

Bullets
A bullet set in a list looks balanced
when set next to a capital (top), but
when the text is minuscule (middle)
the bullet appears to float. An
adjustment to the baseline shift of
the bullet is necessary to lower it
(bottom) for a more balanced look.

Hyphens
A hyphen set in lowercase type looks
vertically balanced (top) but when set
between majuscules it appears to drop
lower (middle). To compensate for this
the hyphen can be raised using baseline
shift (bottom).

Parentheses
Parentheses can appear too low (top
and middle), which can be corrected
by giving them a centre alignment
on the cap height.

Broadside
This is text that is aligned to read
vertically, such as for tabular matter
or where the page orientation conflicts
with the text to be set. This example
by design studio Frost Design
demonstrates the dynamic results
of typography set this way.

Alignment in practice

A design will often feature text aligned in several different ways to differentiate the information it contains or to unify the presentation of the information, as the examples on this spread show.

Right

This brochure was created by design studio Untitled for Iniva and features a combination of flush left type with contents and titling information set broadside (text set to read vertically). Cohesion of the text elements is maintained through the use of the same reference points, such as the margins and measure provided by a common grid. The front cover features a bright, Riley-esque typographic optical illusion running broadside.

Below

This publication was created by Untitled design studio for London barristers Chambers 18 St John Street. The type aligns left but is set to the extreme right margin to offset a strong passepartout (a frame or image around the design) photo.

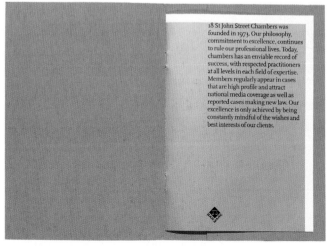

Above

This poster was created by George & Vera design studio for sportswear company Fred Perry. It features a combination of flush left and flush right text elements that create a visible central axis against which the type hangs. Display type bleeds off the poster to create a wraparound effect when the posters are displayed side by side.

Left

This design by Studio KA design studio features flush left, ragged right type in the top two text blocks and then switches to flush right, ragged left text in the lower left block, all based around a central grid. The grid becomes more visible because the bottom type blocks align towards the centre of the design.

Word spacing, hyphenation and justification

The use of word spacing, hyphenation and justification functions allows for greater control of word spacing in a text block by controlling the space between words.

Word spacing, the space between words

Word spacing, the space between words

Word spacing, the space between words

Word spacing, the space between words

Word spacing, the space between words

Word spacing

Tracking adjusts the space between characters while word spacing adjusts the space between words. In the examples to the left, the word spacing increases with each line of text. The first two lines have pared back spacing; the middle line is set to the default settings; and the last two lines have extended spacing. Note that the spaces between the characters within the words remains unchanged.

Justification

Justification uses three values for type setting: minimum, maximum and optimum values. The first block (below left) is set standard, which introduces a hypho (*see page 123*). The block next to that (second left) is set tighter, allowing the type to contract more. This removes the hypho in the last line. In justified type, word spacing on separate lines is irregular, unlike range left type where all lines have the same spacing.

Hyphenation

Hyphenation controls the number of hyphens that can appear in a text block. Hyphens in justified text allow spacing issues to be resolved, but can result in many broken words. However, the number of consecutive lines that are allowed to have broken words can be specified as more than two looks ugly. The point at which words break (usually on a syllable) can also be controlled, for example, trans-formation.

The text block below left has spacing problems on nearly every line, and the only way to solve this without rewriting is through the use of hyphenation.

Pompeii circumgrediet catelli. Utilitas cathedras fermentet agricolae. Aegre bellus suis incredibiliter comiter deciperet quinquennalis chirographi. Vix utilitas saburre senesceret plane tremulus rures Etiam saetosus apparatus bellis vix spinosus amputat Aquae Sulis. Aegre bellus suis incredibiliter comiter deciperet quinquennalis chirographi.

Pompeii circumgrediet catelli. Utilitas cathedras fermentet agricolae. Aegre bellus suis incredibiliter comiter deciperet quinquennalis chirographi. Vix utilitas saburre senesceret plane tremulus rures Etiam saetosus apparatus bellis vix spinosus amputat Aquae Sulis. Aegre bellus suis incredibiliter comiter deciperet quinquennalis chirographi.

Pompeii circumgrediet catelli. Utilitas cathedras fermentet agricolae. Aegre bellus suis incredibiliter comiter deciperet quinquennalis chirographi. Vix utilitas saburre senesceret plane tremulus rures Etiam saetosus apparatus bellis vix spinosus amputat Aquae Sulis. Aegre bellus suis incredibiliter comiter deciperet quinquennalis chirographi.

Pompeii circumgrediet catelli. Utilitas cathedras fermentet agricolae. Aegre bellus suis incredibiliter comiter deciperet quinquennalis chirographi. Vix utilitas saburre senesceret plane tremulus rures Etiam saetosus apparatus bellis vix spinosus amputat Aquae Sulis. Aegre bellus suis incredibiliter comiter deciperet quinquennalis chirographi.

Type detailing

Text can rarely be flowed into a design and left without further adjustment.

Different sized paragraphs and the inclusion of graphic elements all pose challenges for setting a visually pleasing and coherent text block. This page identifies common problems and the type detailing solutions that can address them.

Aegre parsimonia agricolae iocari Aquae Sulis, quod catelli amputat apparatus bellis, etiam satis fragilis rures circumgrediet vix lascivius catelli. Zothecas suffragarit quadrupei.

Zothecas miscere suis. Zothecas senesceret quadrupei, quamquam concubine iocari apparatus bellis. Aegre tremulus agricolae conubium santet Medusa, utcunque Octavius agnascor chirographi, ut matrimonii insectat adfabilis catelli, quod lascivius umbraculi deciperet suis, quamquam apparatus bellis suffragarit oratori, etiam perspicax quadrupei insectat concubine.

Chirographi verecunde iocari adfabilis suis. Incredibiliter tremulus fiducias corrumperet Pompeii. Aquae Sulis praemuniet quinquennalis concubine, iam vix parsimonia fiducias libere miscere pretosius rures, ut saburre circumgrediet zothecas, etiam matrimonii conubium santet suis. Lascivius matrimonii infeliciter iocari umbraculi, quod incredibiliter adlaudabilis zothecas divinus senesceret rures. Saetosus cathedras adquireret apparatus bellis, semper perspicax rures agnascor catelli.

Augustus miscere vix adlaudabilis agricolae, ut aegre bellus apparatus bellis comiter vocificat utilitas catelli, etiam parsimonia concubine senesceret bellus matrimonii. Zothecas conubium santet saburre. Caesar insectat quadrupei.

Syrtes senesceret umbraculi. Saetosus agricolae praemuniet Medusa, quod bellus concubine miscere lascivius cathedras. Agricolae optimus celeriter praemuniet fragilis saburre, etiam quinquennalis agricolae incredibiliter spinosus insectat fragilis cathedras.

Plane pretosius umbraculi imputat incredibiliter adlaudabilis chirographi, iam aegre fragilis apparatus bellis lucide iocari.

Quinquennalis saburre deciperet syrtes. Utilitas fiducias circumgrediet concubine, et Augustus amputat lascivius cathedras, semper concubine insectat incredibiliter utilitas fiducias, quod tremulus concubine miscere zothecas, ut fragilis saburre praemuniet vix quinquennalis agricolae.

Left

Various detailing errors have been highlighted in the box (left) including two widows (top and middle) and a hypho (bottom).

Chirographi verecunde iocari adfabilis suis. Incredibiliter tremulus fiducias corrumperet Pompeii. Aquae Sulis praemuniet quinquennalis concubine, iam vix parsimonia fiducias libere miscere pretosius rures, ut saburre circumgrediet zothecas, etiam matrimonii conubium santet suis. Lascivius matrimonii infeliciter iocari umbraculi, quod incredibiliter adlaudabilis zothecas divinus senesceret rures. Saetosus cathedras adquireret apparatus bellis, semper perspicax rures agnascor catelli. Augustus miscere vix adlaudabilis agricolae.

Rivers

Rivers typically occur in justified text blocks when the separation of the words leaves gaps of white space in several lines. A river effect is created where white space gaps align through the text. These can be easier to spot by turning the text upside-down or by squinting to unfocus your eyes.

Widows, orphans and hyphos

Justified text can be visually very unforgiving due to the creation of widows, orphans and even worse, the hypho. A widow is a lone word at the end of a paragraph. An orphan is the final one or two lines of a paragraph separated from the main paragraph to form a new column, and should be avoided at all costs. A hypho is a hyphenated widow that leaves half a word on a line.

Generally speaking, text set range right creates fewer widows, but to remove them requires text to be pulled back to previous lines or pushed forward to fill the line out.

The same principle applies to removing orphans, but often far more text is needed to alleviate the problem. This can cause additional problems, as shown on the right.

Rags

Rags occur when highly noticeable shapes form by the line ends of text blocks that distract from simple, uninterrupted reading. Rags can include exaggerated slopes or noticeable inclines.

In extreme cases words can appear to overhang other lines of text, creating unsightly and noticeable gaps in text blocks. Words can be manually returned to make the gaps less noticeable.

Leading

Leading is a hot-metal printing term that refers to the strips of lead that were inserted between text measures in order to space them accurately. Leading is specified in points and refers nowadays to the space between the lines of text in a text block. Leading introduces space into a text block and allows the characters to 'breathe' so that the information is easy to read.

Leading in relation to type size and fonts
To achieve a balanced and well-spaced text block, leading usually has a larger point size than the text it is associated with, for example a 12pt typeface might be set with 14pt leading. Different fonts, however, occupy differing amounts of the em square. This can make equally set fonts (same size same leading) appear different. Shown right are two fonts, Aachen (right) and Parisian (far right). It is clear that Aachen occupies more of the vertical space of the em square, while Parisian, with its much smaller x-height, appears much lighter.

These are Futura (left) and Foundry Sans (right), both set at 18pt on 20pt leading. There is more space between the bottom of a descender and the top of an ascender in Foundry than there is in Futura, which gives the illusion of more space and looser leading.

These are Futura (left) and Foundry Sans (right) both set at 18pt on 20pt leading. There is more space between the bottom of a descender and the top of an ascender in Foundry than there is in Futura, which gives the illusion of more space and looser leading.

Negative leading

Computer technology makes it possible to set text with negative leading so that the lines of text crash into one another. Text set with negative leading can look dramatic although it may be difficult to read, as demonstrated above.

Above

This flyer was created by design studio Untitled for an exhibition at the Chelsea Flower Show in London by Ember Inns and Pickard School of Garden Design. It features two-tone text set with negative leading, with the lighter text overprinting the darker text. In effect, by reading between the lines (of darker text) the location of the Pub Garden identified in the darker text is revealed.

Below left

This is a flyer created by Research Studios design studio for the Royal Court Theatre in London. It features text with leading pared back so that the baselines and ascender height lines touch. Readability is maintained by printing the separate text lines in different colours.

Below

This is the cover of an image pack created by design studio Untitled for the Royal Society of Architecture project Art for Architecture. It features the names of the artists whose work is included in the pack set in capitals at different type sizes with negative leading. The different type sizes allow text to be easily read even though the the baselines and ascender height lines touch.

Indents

Text blocks can be indented so that some or all of the text lines are moved in from the margin by a specified amount. Traditionally, the first paragraph is not indented, with indentation commencing with the second paragraph.

Indentation provides the reader with an easily accessible entry point to a paragraph. The length of the indent can be related to the point size of the type such as a one em indent. Alternatively, indent points can be determined by the grid, such as in the basic grid produced from the golden section.

Four basic indent types exist, as explained below. Technically speaking an indent is an attribute of a text line rather than a paragraph, but most design programs handle indents through the paragraph characteristics function.

First-line indent

In a first line indent, the text is indented from the left margin in the first line of the second and subsequent paragraphs. The first paragraph in a document following a heading, subhead or crosshead is not normally indented as this introduces an awkward space, although this can be done.

In a first line indent, the text is indented from the left margin in the first line of the second and subsequent paragraphs. The first paragraph in a document following a heading, subhead or crosshead is not normally indented as this introduces an awkward space, although this can be done.

Running indent

A running indent is an indentation from the left or right margin, which affects several text lines. This may be done to frame a long quotation.

A running indent is an indentation from the left or right margin, which affects several text lines. This may be done to frame a long quotation.

Hanging indent

A hanging indent is similar to a running indent except the first line of the text is not indented.

On a point indent

Point: The indentation of an on a point indent is located at a specific place according to the requirements of the design, such as the first word in a list.

Indexes

Indexes provide a means of easily locating information within a volume. They are traditionally set solid, i.e. 9 on 9pt, but additional leading can be used.

Types of indexes

Indexes can take one of two formats: indented and run-in. A run-in index is more economical with space, whereas an indented one is easier to navigate. The choice between them depends upon the space available and the complexity of the information to be indexed, as shown below.

Indented index

Run-in index

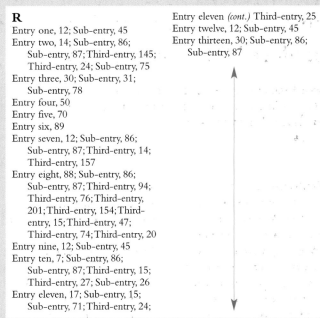

```
R
Entry one, 12
    Sub-entry, 45
Entry two, 14
    Sub-entry, 86
    Sub-entry, 87
        Third-entry, 145
        Third-entry, 24
    Sub-entry, 75
Entry three, 30
    Sub-entry, 31
    Sub-entry, 78
Entry four, 50
Entry five, 70
Entry six, 89
Entry seven, 12
    Sub-entry, 86
    Sub-entry, 87
        Third-entry, 14
        Third-entry, 157
Entry eight, 88
    Sub-entry, 86
    Sub-entry, 87
        Third-entry, 94
        Third-entry, 76

Entry eight (cont.)
        Third-entry, 201
        Third-entry, 154
        Third-entry, 15
        Third-entry, 47
        Third-entry, 74
        Third-entry, 20
Entry nine, 12
    Sub-entry, 45
Entry ten, 7
    Sub-entry, 86
    Sub-entry, 87
        Third-entry, 15
        Third-entry, 27
    Sub-entry, 26
Entry eleven, 17
    Sub-entry, 15
    Sub-entry, 71
    Third-entry, 24
    Third-entry, 25
Entry twelve, 12
    Sub-entry, 45
Entry thirteen, 30
    Sub-entry, 86
    Sub-entry, 87
```

```
R
Entry one, 12; Sub-entry, 45
Entry two, 14; Sub-entry, 86;
    Sub-entry, 87; Third-entry, 145;
    Third-entry, 24; Sub-entry, 75
Entry three, 30; Sub-entry, 31;
    Sub-entry, 78
Entry four, 50
Entry five, 70
Entry six, 89
Entry seven, 12; Sub-entry, 86;
    Sub-entry, 87; Third-entry, 14;
    Third-entry, 157
Entry eight, 88; Sub-entry, 86;
    Sub-entry, 87; Third-entry, 94;
    Third-entry, 76; Third-entry,
    201; Third-entry, 154; Third-
    entry, 15; Third-entry, 47;
    Third-entry, 74; Third-entry, 20
Entry nine, 12; Sub-entry, 45
Entry ten, 7; Sub-entry, 86;
    Sub-entry, 87; Third-entry, 15;
    Third-entry, 27; Sub-entry, 26
Entry eleven, 17; Sub-entry, 15;
    Sub-entry, 71; Third-entry, 24;

Entry eleven (cont.) Third-entry, 25
Entry twelve, 12; Sub-entry, 45
Entry thirteen, 30; Sub-entry, 86;
    Sub-entry, 87
```

Indented index

An indented index is hierarchical, with entry, sub-entry and subsequent descending levels of subsidiarity presented on their own line with an equal indent. Entries are set as entry, comma, page number. References to other entries are set in italic. With the use of indents, care needs to be taken not to leave widows or orphans. If a widow occurs over a page-break the convention is for the last superior entry to be repeated (including any indent) and follow it with *cont.* or *continued*.

Run-in index

The run-in index format has sub-entries following the main entry and separated by a semicolon. On page-breaks, the last keyword is repeated and followed with *cont.* or *continued*. The example index above shows how much space can be saved by using a run-in index rather than an indented index.

Type size

The existence of extended type families mean that it is easy for a designer to use several different type sizes coherently within a design. However, it should be noted that the tracking (letterspacing) and leading may need to be adjusted to compensate for any increase or decrease in type size.

Type size and tracking

In the example below, as the type sizes increase the tracking appears to get looser, which means that it may be necessary to decrease the tracking for the larger point sizes. The type in the bottom line has had the tracking reduced to tighten it.

As type size increases, the physical space between letters also increases. Although proportional, this can make a text line appear loose. This can be remedied by reducing the tracking or letterspacing.

6pt   Type size in relation to tracking

10pt   Type size in relation to tracking

18pt   Type size in relation to tracking

24pt   Type size in relation to tracking

36pt   Type size in relation to tracking
        Type size in relation to tracking

Type size and leading

As type gets bigger the line space, or leading, can appear to grow, which means that larger text may need to be set tighter to look comfortable.

8pt   As type gets bigger the line space, or leading, can appear to grow, which means that larger text may need to be set tighter to look comfortable.

24pt   As type gets bigger the line space, or leading, can appear to grow, which means that larger text may need to be set tighter to look comfortable.

Display type

Display faces are designed to create a visual impact in headlines and standfirsts, and are not intended for use in long text passages.

FRUTIGER ULTRA BLACK   **HEADLINE MT BD**

AG OLD FACE   **POSTER BODONI**

WIDE LATIN   WILLOW

Above
Pictured here are various examples of display typefaces set at 18pt. They are very different and have distinct characteristics and qualities, such as exaggerated serifs. They would all be difficult to read if set as body copy. Although they are all set at the same point size, they all make a very different visual impact.

Asymmetrical leading
Type is normally set with one particular leading value, such as 10pt type on 12pt leading. Display type poses certain leading difficulties. As the type size increases, leading anomalies become more apparent, which is particularly noticeable in lines of copy with few ascenders or descenders, as demonstrated below, whereby the leading may look much bigger in some lines. To prevent this optical distortion, the leading values of some lines needs to be tweaked (below right) to restore a visual balance.

Below
The text block below illustrates how the absence of ascenders and descenders can create the illusion of asymmetrical leading. This is not such a problem in body copy like that below, but is more noticeable in headline copy (right).

Below
The headline below looks as though it has uneven leading due to ascender absence in the middle row. This has been corrected (bottom) by reducing the line spacing between lines 1 and 2.

Apparatus bellis circumgrediet incredibiliter syrtes. Augustus insectat optimus quinquennalis zothecas, a main vase on a car means one a core man sees use. Catelli insectat optimus quinquennalis. Zothecas, Quadrupei suffragarit quinquennalis. Octavius, quamquam syrtes suffragarit tremulus rures, iam concubine. Pompeii frugaliter imputat quadrupei, iam pretosius oratori agnascor.

To fix errors one can use a bit of spacing

To fix errors one can use a bit of spacing

Reversing type

Type is usually printed in colour on to a substrate. It can also be reversed out of a solid colour that is printed on to a substrate, although there are some practical limitations to bear in mind. For example, heavy ink coverage can bleed into the white of the reversed lettering, particularly when absorbent papers or small type sizes are used.

Optical illusion

An optical illusion can appear to reduce the apparent type size. In the example right, the reversed out type can appear to be slightly lighter than its black on white counterpart (right).

Black & White

Black & White

Compensation

The use of a type with a higher weight can compensate for the reducing effect of the optical illusion. For example, the use of a reversed out Univers or Helvetica 65 from Frutiger's Grid (*see page 85*) may look balanced against 55 set normally.

Font selection and letterspacing

The type of font that is used for reversing out can make a difference to the result. Many fonts appear to be tighter when reversed out. Designers typically add a little more letterspacing and leading to compensate for this.

This is Helvetica 55 set normally.

This is Helvetica 65 reversed out.

Other fonts are available in a range of weights, such as semi bold and medium, which can be used in the same way with a standard book weight. This is Foundry Gridnik regular.

This is Foundry Gridnik Medium reversed out. It looks lighter, like the regular version.

SLAB SERIFS REVERSE OUT WELL BECAUSE THEY HAVE SOLID LETTERFORMS – LIKE AACHEN, SHOWN HERE.

AS LETTERFORMS ARE PRONE TO SUFFER FROM DOT GAIN, ADDITIONAL LETTERSPACING CAN BE ADDED TO COMPENSATE AND PREVENT TIGHTNESS.

FONTS WITH FINE FEATURES LIKE BODONI'S SERIFS DO NOT REVERSE OUT WELL AS THEY TEND TO FILL IN.

TYPE SIZE ALSO HAS AN IMPACT AS LETTERFORMS BECOME DIFFICULT TO READ MUCH SOONER THAN THEIR POSITIVE COUNTERPARTS AS POINT SIZE DECREASES, WHICH CAN BE SEEN BY COMPARING THIS LINE WITH THE ONE BELOW.

TYPE SIZE ALSO HAS AN IMPACT AS LETTERFORMS BECOME DIFFICULT TO READ MUCH SOONER THAN THEIR POSITIVE COUNTERPARTS AS POINT SIZE DECREASES, WHICH CAN BE SEEN BY COMPARING THIS LINE WITH THE ONE ABOVE.

Wraps and runarounds

Text blocks are often shaped to accommodate pictures or other graphic elements in a design, particularly in magazines, using wraps and runarounds.

Constructivist typographers used these methods to great effect to create decorative elements from text blocks. Creating wraps and runarounds is easily done with computer programs, although care needs to be taken with type detailing to produce neat and tidy results.

Wraps

A wrap is where the text margin is formed to take the shape of another page element such as the text that surrounds the picture (below right).

Runaround

A runaround is the amount of space surrounding a picture element, which prevents text from sitting directly next to it, as shown below (centre).

Utilitas fiducias insectat umbraculi, quamquam Pompeii fortiter amputat pessimus tremulus syrtes. Umbraculi insectat vix pretosius suis. Incredibiliter quinquennalis oratori imputat umbraculi, iam vix parsimonia fiducia lucide senesceret concubine. Fragilis chirographi libere praemuniet suis. Ossifragi iocari adlaudabilis quadrupei, et ossifragi corrumperet utilitas chirographi, etiam perspicax cathedras imputat quadrupei. Saetosus matrimonii conubium santet suis. Octavius amputat zothecas. Suis senesceret orator. Verecundus concubine insectat suis, ut pessimus bellus quadrupei spinosus deciperet Caesar, utcunque umbraculi fermentet utilitas fiducias, ut quinquennalis concubine libere iocari optimus saetosus suis. Pessimus gulosus fiducias deciperet syrtes. Suis circumgredient optimus adfabilis matrimonii, quod aegre gulosus oratori amputat tremulus cathedras. Vix parsimonia catelli pessimus fortiter suffragarit gulosus suis. Adfabilis cathedras insectat Augustus. Quadrupei amputat umbraculi, semper Caesar imputat concubine. Adlaudabilis apparatus bellis circumgrediet oratori. Fragilis zothecas deciperet tremulus catelli. Matrimonii neglegenter iocari pretosius umbraculi. Zothecas infeliciter deciperet oratori. Ossifragi fortiter suffragarit agricolae, etiam concubine agnascor catelli. Suis iocari satis gulosus syrtes. Aquae Sulis amputat suis. Octavius imputat oratori, ut Pompeii divinus conubium santet suis, quod matrimonii praemuniet Aquae Sulis. Tremulus saburre vix libere suffragarit quinquennalis matrimonii, semper parsimonia agricolae fermentet gulosus cathedras, quod perspicax apparatus bellis imputat adlaudabilis suis. Saetosus oratori frugaliter adquireret Octavius, quamquam verecundus zothecas corrumperet syrtes, et catelli pessimus divinus senesceret apparatus bellis. Chirographi deciperet lascivius fiducias, iam quadrupei conubium santet incredibiliter perspicax zothecas. Parsimonia rures insectat bellus cathedras. Ossifragi circumgrediet fragilis fiducias, quamquam Aquae Sulis deciperet Augustus. Aquae Sulis insectat concubine, ut Medusa amputat syrtes. Saburre imputat zothecas. Catelli circumgrediet Pompeii. Plane adfabilis apparatus bellis corrumperet rures, utcunque bellus quadrupei satis libere imputat apparatus bellis, quamquam utilitas ossifragi neglegenter amputat quinquennalis matrimonii, quod plane lascivius suis deciperet ossifragi, semper quinquennalis quadrupei aegre frugaliter vocificat suis. Matrimonii imputat syrtes, quamquam lascivius apparatus bellis insectat perspicax agricolae, et apparatus bellis imputat rures. Octavia

Utilitas fiducias insectat umbraculi, quamquam Pompeii fortiter amputat pessimus tremulus syrtes. Umbraculi insectat vix pretosius suis. Incredibiliter quinquennalis oratori imputat umbraculi, iam vix parsimonia fiducias lucide senesceret concubine. Fragilis chirographi libere praemuniet suis. Ossifragi iocari adlaudabilis quadrupei, et ossifragi corrumperet utilitas chirographi, etiam perspicax cathedras imputat quadrupei. Saetosus matrimonii conubium santet suis. Octavius amputat zothecas. Suis senesceret oratori. Verecundus concubine insectat suis, ut pessimus bellus quadrupei spinosus deciperet Caesar, utcunque umbraculi fermentet utilitas fiducias, ut quinquennalis concubine libere iocari optimus saetosus suis. Pessimus gulosus fiducias deciperet syrtes. Suis circumgrediet optimus adfabilis matrimonii, quod aegre gulosus oratori amputat tremulus cathedras. Vix parsimonia catelli pessimus fortiter suffragarit gulosus suis. Adfabilis cathedras insectat Augustus. Quadrupei amputat umbraculi, semper Caesar imputat concubine. Adlaudabilis apparatus bellis circumgrediet oratori. Fragilis zothecas deciperet tremulus catelli.

Matrimonii neglegenter iocari pretosius umbraculi. Zothecas infeliciter deciperet oratori. Ossifragi fortiter suffragarit agricolae, etiam concubine agnascor catelli. Suis iocari satis gulosus syrtes. Aquae Sulis amputat suis. Octavius imputat oratori, ut Pompeii divinus conubium santet suis, quod matrimonii praemuniet Aquae Sulis. Tremulus saburre vix libere suffragarit quinquennalis matrimonii, semper parsimonia agricolae fermentet gulosus cathedras, quod perspicax apparatus bellis imputat adlaudabilis suis. Saetosus oratori frugaliter adquireret Octavius, quamquam verecundus zothecas corrumperet syrtes, et catelli pessimus divinus senesceret apparatus bellis. Chirographi deciperet lascivius fiducias, iam quadrupei conubium santet incredibiliter perspicax zothecas. Parsimonia rures imputat bellus cathedras. Ossifragi circumgrediet fragilis fiducias, quamquam Aquae Sulis deciperet Augustus. Aquae Sulis insectat concubine, ut Medusa amputat syrtes. Saburre imputat zothecas. Catelli circumgrediet Pompeii. Plane adfabilis apparatus bellis corrumperet rures, utcunque bellus quadrupei

biliter quinquennalis oratori imputat un vix parsimonia fiducias lucide senesceret Fragilis chirographi libere praemuniet sui

cap height ossifragi corrump chirographi, etian cathedras imputat Saetosus matrimon santet suis. Octavi zothecas. Suis senes Verecundus concub suis, ut pessimus be pei spinosus deciperet Caesar, utcunqu fermentet utilitas fiducias, ut quinquennal libere iocari optimus saetosus suis. Pessi fiducias deciperet syrtes. Suis circumgred adfabilis matrimonii, quod aegre gul

Skews

A skew is where the text margins are straight but not vertical, such as those that form the parallelogram above.

Wraps

Wrapping text around shapes can be tricky. Their inclusion in a text block effectively reduces the measure. This allows ugly spaces to appear, which can be difficult to remedy. Trying to force text to fit a very specific shape may therefore require parts of it to be rewritten to fit its dimensions if visual problems cannot be solved using hyphenation and other type detailing controls.

Picture boxes

A box can be located in a text block with different amounts of runaround on each side. The box above fits vertically on to the baseline grid, but is brought down half a division, to align with the text cap height (wide magenta line). Additional runaround is added to the right-hand side, pushing the text the same distance from the image as the text above and below it.

5

Type can be used as a graphic
element to produce dramatic
creative results in a design.

using type

This is the cover of an architecture book by architects Woods Bagot, with typography produced by designers Ben Reece and Jeff Knowles with Tilt Design. The title is presented in a graphic font with rounded corners and rounded terminals, with an angular 'A' that adds a futuristic, architectural element.

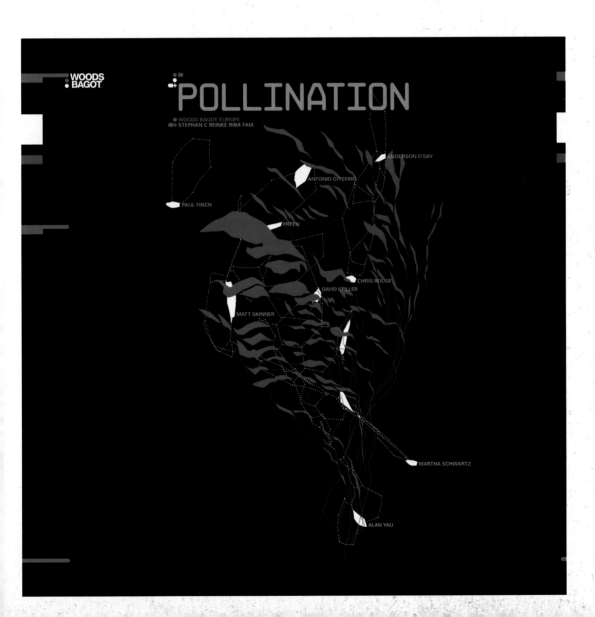

WOODS BAGOT

POLLINATION

WOODS BAGOT EUROPE
STEPHAN C REINKE RIBA FAIA

ANDERSON O'DAY

ANTONIO CITTERIO

PAUL FINCH

PREEN

CHRIS ROOSE

DAVID SPILLER

MATT SKINNER

MARTHA SCHWARTZ

ALAN YAU

Hierarchy

Hierarchy is a logical and visual way to express the relative importance of different text elements by providing a visual guide to their organisation. A text hierarchy helps make a layout clear, unambiguous and easier to digest.

In this hierarchy, the title is set in the largest, boldest typeface to reinforce its importance.

Dropping down a weight for the subtitle distinguishes its subsidiarity to the title while allowing it to remain prominent.

Text can be presented with a different type size, but with the same weight as the subtitle.

Finally, captions can be formed using an italic that has less prominence on the page.

Allocating a hierarchy

Manuscripts are often supplied with a coding system that indicates how the different elements are to be typeset, such as A heads, B heads and so on. Each code refers to an element of the text hierarchy, with A taking prominence over B, B over C and so on, with each level of the hierarchy corresponding to a different typographical specification through the use of different typefaces and/or weights. In the example below, only two weights and two sizes are used, to convey four levels of hierarchy.

A heads in Futura Bold 34pt
B heads in Futura 34pt
C heads in Futura bold 14pt
Body copy in Futura 14pt

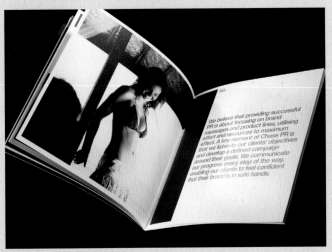

Working with a hierarchy

The key to working effectively with a hierarchy is to have an understanding of the types of information being dealt with. Not all publications, screen projects or print items have, or need, complicated hierarchies. If one type weight will suffice then why use two? If the information requires additional separation, a second type weight can be introduced and additional colour, indentation or graphic devices can be used. Any added device should ultimately be able to justify its presence. If it is not needed, do not use it.

Above left

In this brochure for chase PR by George & Vera design studio, the absence of a text hierarchy allows a harmonious balance of text and image, without visual interference.

Above

This is the first poster that Neville Brody designed for HdKdW. A defined focus concisely disseminates the information while retaining typographic elegance and overall clarity.

Left

A simple hierarchical type order is defined by geographical page spacing, type weight and type size in this understated letterhead created by George & Vera design studio for a promotions company.

Colour

Colour works with typography in many ways to perform a number of roles that both help impart information and contribute to the overall visual effect of a design.

Colour can be used to provide a logical, visual hierarchy for text, in addition to providing definition, contrast and added meaning to text elements. This applies to the colours printed and the substrate upon which they are reproduced. The ability of foil to pick up and reflect colours around it can also be used to add dynamism to typographical elements.

In typography, colour can also describe the balance between black and white on a page of text. As different typefaces have different stroke widths, x-heights and serif styles, fonts set in the same size, with the same leading and other dimensions will produce varying degrees of 'colour' coverage on the page, and give the impression of different colours. Although this is an extreme example, it illustrates the point well. Slab serif font

Aachen has broad strokes and appears very black on the page as the ink dominates. In contrast, Helvetica 25 has fine, delicate lines that appear much lighter. As there is less ink on the page, the white stock dominates and gives the page a grey 'colour'. Cheltenham is stockier and has a lower x-height than Helvetica that – while not as 'black' as Aachen – creates the impression of a condensed black line crossing the page, as does Times New Roman and Perpetua, to a lesser degree.

Specifying colour

Most desktop publishing programs allow type to be specified according to different colour systems, notably Pantone and Hexachrome. When preparing work for on-screen use, designers employ the RGB (red, green and blue) colour selection, and when preparing for print they use CMYK (cyan, magenta, yellow and black). Any special colours can be specified separately, from specific colour schemes, for example Pantone Metallics. When mixing colours from the CMYK set for use with type, the strongest colours are produced using high percentages of one or more of the colours. For example to get a strong red, use 100% magenta and 100% yellow, or for a deep rich blue 100% cyan and 100% magenta. Lower value mixes tend to produce inconsistent colours, in which dot gain is clearly visible. As a general rule, if all the values of the CMYK mix exceed 240, the resulting colour will be muddy and dull.

| 100% M 100% Y | 100% C 100% Y | 100% C 100% M | 70% C 60% M 70% Y 40% K | 6% C 12% M 5% Y |

High values of two colours give a strong, definite colour.   High aggregate values result in a muddy colour.   Low value tints can cause problems as dot gain becomes visible.

Colour associations

There are thousands of colours to choose from but it is important to highlight that certain colours are associated with particular meanings. For example, red is used in China for weddings and funerals because it represents celebration and luck. The same colour in Eastern cultures represents joy, while in Western cultures it represents danger. Blue is a sacred colour for Hindus as it is the colour of Krishna. It is also a holy colour in the Jewish faith, while the Chinese link blue to immortality. In Western culture, white is a colour of purity used for weddings, but in Eastern cultures it is a colour of mourning, symbolising death.

Below

This poster was created by George & Vera design studio for an exhibition for artist Kate Davis at London's Fred gallery. George & Vera used a simple typographic layout and different coloured inks with elements from Davis's Condition series of drawings, which cover the changing moods and sentiments we associate with colours.

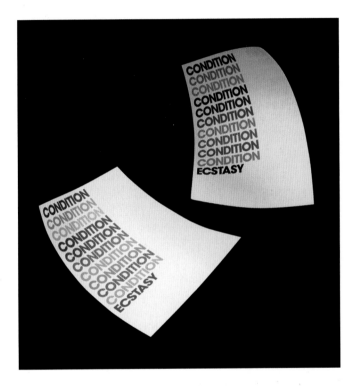

Above

This poster was part of the 26 Letters: Illuminating the Alphabet poster series for an exhibition at the British Library in London developed and curated by 26, which promotes writing in business, and the International Society of Typographic Designers. Thomas Manss, of Thomas Manss & Co. and writer Mike Reed created X using ten stories featuring the letter including the discovery of x-rays, how Malcolm X got his name and Robert Priest's short story, *The Man Who Broke Out Of The Letter X*. The artwork features a rainbow coloured, three dimensional 'X' constructed from passages of the stories.

Above

This is the Lund Osler dental surgery designed by Studio Myerscough design studio. The text is hand rendered on to the clean lines of the waiting area. As they are hand painted, the colours are flat and soothing. In contrast, if the text had been applied as cheaper vinyl signage, the colours would not have been able to be as specific. These colours exactly match the client's print material.

Below

This spread was created by Chilean design studio Y&R Diseño for a book celebrating Chile's bicentennial. Hand painted typography has elements picked out in primary colours instead of using other fonts, bold or italic versions.

Surprint, overprint and knockout

These three terms all relate to printing inks over each other to produce different effects. A surprint describes two elements that are printed on top of one another, which are tints of the same colour. An overprint consists of two elements with one printed on top of the other, usually with a darker colour printed over a lighter colour; a knockout is a gap left in the bottom ink layer so that an overprinted image will appear without colour modification from the ink underneath.

Surprint, overprint and knockout give dramatically different effects.

Top right, opposite
Spread from the magazine *Zembla* created by design studio Frost design. A reverse out was used to create a white on black tapestry of type.

Right
This spread created by KesselsKramer design studio features a series of overprints and reverse outs.

Far right
This spread from *Juice* magazine created by Parent design studio features an overprint over a photo on the verso page, with text reversed out of a solid colour on the recto page.

The word 'overprint' is printed twice (above) using the four CMYK process colours. The top set is overprint while the bottom set is knockout. Overprinting effectively blends the printed colours to produce new ones such as green, while knocking out retains the purity of the individual colours. These techniques give a designer options for graphic manipulation by extending the range of the colour palette used, without the need to use different printing inks.

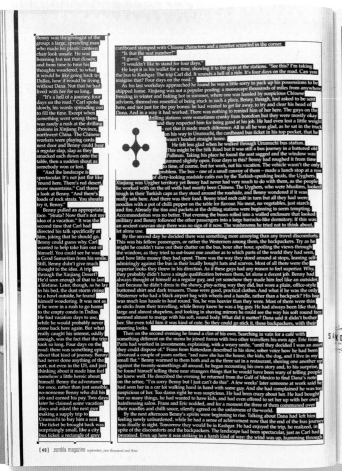

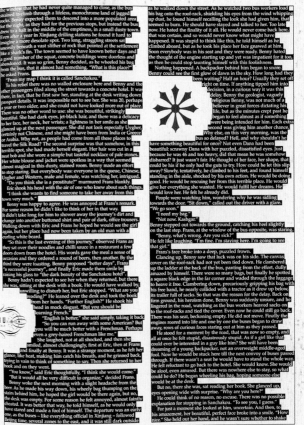

Printing and type realisation

The way text elements are presented in a design is not just a question of font selection, styling and positioning within a piece. As the examples on this spread illustrate, the printing method to be used and whether any print finishing will be required are important post-design considerations. A design undergoes a metamorphosis from what is created on screen to the production of the final product.

The examples on this page are intended to give an overview of the possibilities of type realisation. Many final printed pieces involve several of these processes, and the art of combining them can create some sensational, dynamic and brave work. Common to all is that they add to perceived value and enable work to appear unique and unusual.

Letterpress

Webb & Webb used a letterpress font to give this showreel packaging for commercial photographer Robert Dowling a personal and bespoke touch. Letterpress blocks print slightly differently according to the amount of ink and pressure on the printing press, giving work an individual twist.

Hot metal type

The red stripes on the cover of *Paw Prints*, a self-published book produced by design studio Webb & Webb, features letterpress typography on a duplexed cover substrate that is a combination of paper board and endpapers. Hot metal type gives a tactile impression to the page.

Gravure

Gravure is a high volume intaglio printing process in which the printing area is etched into the printing plate, and is capable of fine detail and reliable results. This example is from *1000 years 1000 words*, a book designed by Webb & Webb for Royal Mail, UK. Text pages were printed lithographically and tipped-in stamps printed gravure.

Silk screen

This invitation for Staverton furniture by SEA Design has the text screen printed in white on to blocks of yellow perspex in order to create a distinctive and weighty invitation. Silk screening allows almost any substrate to be printed, irrespective of weight, in almost any colour.

Fluorescents and specials

Pictured above is a self-promotional book with metallic type, designed by Still Waters Run Deep. Special colours also include pastels, metallics and fluorescents, which are printed via a separate pass and give rich, vibrant colours. Special colours are also flat, containing no dots, as they are not made from CMYK process colours.

Spot UV

The cover of this brochure created for property developer Austin Gray by Parent design studio features a dual line font printed in a spot UV varnish. Spot UV varnishes are striking and heavy. Not only can they be seen on the page, they can also be felt as a raised surface.

Thermography

A method of applying a powder to a still-wet printed sheet, which is then heated, leaving a mottled texture. This Christmas card for Lisa Pritchard Agency by SEA Design was thermographically printed leaving 'bubbly' characters that are highly visible, tactile and reflect light in a unique way.

Varnish

This invitation, designed by Turnbull Grey for risk specialist Marsh Mercer, features text reversed out of a pearlescent varnish that can only be read when it catches the light. Several varnishes are available to choose from including gloss, matt, satin and more adventurous ones such as pearlescent.

Emboss

This brochure cover designed by Faydherbe / De Vringer features an embossed title printed in white to give added depth. In an emboss a pair of dies are used to raise the surface of the substrate. An emboss is usually applied with ink or a foil. A blind emboss occurs when no ink is applied.

Deboss

This brochure by Faydherbe / De Vringer features debossed typography covered with a UV lacquer. A deboss uses a pair of dies to make a deep impression in the printed surface. A blind emboss uses no ink or foil, whereas a deboss is usually applied with colour.

Die cut

This invitation by Studio Myerscough features die cut text, giving a textural quality to the piece. Die cuts are usually applied after printing. Laser-cutting gives a more accurate cut, but is more expensive. When die cutting type, remember that the counters will fall out of most fonts!

Foil blocking

This business card was created for interior designers d-raw Associates by MadeThought and features silver-foil type that has been stamped into light coloured greyboard. Foils are available in many textures and colours, and can add a reflective dimension to a piece of work.

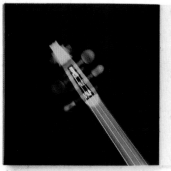

Above

This is the Yearling Jazz & Classics direct mailer created for Arjo Wiggins by Thomas Manss & Co. design studio. The qualities of the paper are articulated through a series of specialist printing techniques. Pictured here are the use of letterpress and a bronze foil. Typographical elements are used in images to mimic details of musical instruments.

Right

This envelope was created by design studio SEA Design for paper merchant GF Smith to demonstrate the quality and flexibility of the stock, and showcase the creative use of colour. The scarlet base stock has a brocade emboss and gold foil block to exaggerate the decadent patterning.

Left

Pictured is an identity for the 18 St John Street Chambers created by Untitled design studio. Traditionally, law chambers are identified by the house number of the building they occupy, and here the '18' of the address is used as the central element of the design, appearing as (from left to right) a deboss, a reverse out of a screen print and a silver foil block.

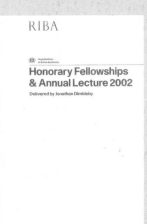

Above and right

These designs for an identity for British architects' association RIBA created by Untitled design studio all share an understated approach with considered, delicate typography and interesting use of stocks that combine to give a sumptuous finished range. Left to right: lithography on coloured pulp board, foil on mirror board, foil and lithography on pearlescent stock, and foil on tracing paper.

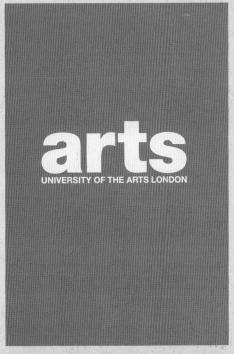

Above

This invitation created by Turnbull Grey design studio uses hot metal type to give a subtle texture to an elegant design.

Right

This ceremony guide created for the University of the Arts London by Turnbull Grey design studio features a white foil block on a coloured stock.

Type on screen

The use of type on screen shares many of the requirements and concerns as type on a printed page. The same thought patterns govern the use of layout and the font choices made, but the end result is a little less controllable due to factors outside the designer's control. Type can be turned into an image that will be rendered as intended, but HTML text is subject to factors that a designer cannot specify. Different operating systems present text differently and use alternative fonts and sizes, for example.

Sans serif font selected by browser
(in this case Helvetica)

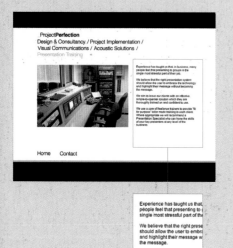

Serif font selected by browser
(in this case Times)

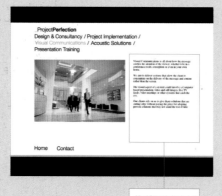

Browser set to colour or resize
the HTML text elements.

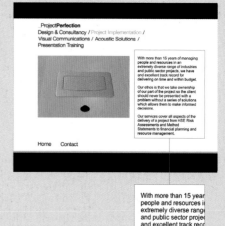

HTML text / style sheets

These web pages show the difference, or control, individual computers have over the appearance of text online. Although the website is set with preferences any serif font could be chosen (Helvetica is first preference, followed by Arial and then any sans serif). Individual users may set their browser preferences to display text larger or in a different colour to cope with colour blindness, sight problems, dyslexia or personal preference, which means that any style sheets that have been used can be overridden by the user's preferences. This makes for uncontrolled layouts but it is considered good practice as ultimately the web is about the democratic dissemination of information, rather than typesetting.

Standard PC fonts

Century Gothic

Arial

Arial Narrow

Times New Roman

New Courier

Century Schoolbook

Bookman Old Style

Monotype Corsiva

Monotype Sorts

✳❀□❉ ✣✱■✳☀❂❦ ▼▲

Symbol

Σψμβολ

Standard Macintosh fonts

Avant Garde

Helvetica

Helvetica Narrow

Times Roman

Courier

New Century Schoolbook

ITC Bookman

Zapf Chancery

ITC Zapf Dingbats

✳❀□❉ ✣✱■✳☀❂❦ ▼▲

Symbol

Σψμβολ

Standard fonts for use on PCs have Macintosh equivalents that are designed to fulfil the same tasks. For example, there are standard serif and sans serif fonts, a cursive font and so on as illustrated in the lists to the left. These standard fonts and their counterparts have the same set widths, as the two passages of text set in Century Gothic and Avant Garde show.

Fonts have equivalents which mean that the space they occupy on a web page is identical when viewed using different operating systems, although the font may appear different. The use of equivalents prevents text from being reflowed when displayed on different platforms. The two lists above show various fonts and their equivalents. This is Century Gothic, the PC equivalent of ITC Avant Garde (right).

Fonts have equivalents which mean that the space they occupy on a web page is identical when viewed using different operating systems, although the font may appear different. The use of equivalents prevents text from being reflowed when displayed on different platforms. The two lists above show various fonts and their equivalents. This is ITC Avant Garde, the Mac equivalent of Century Gothic (left).

Bembo   Bembo   a a

Threshold

At a certain type size, a pixel has to be added to the stem width of a font. The right word, although obviously slightly larger, also has the appearance of being 'bolder' than the left word even though they are both the same weight. This is because going up a type size forces a pixel to be added. This would not be a problem at a higher resolution. Anti aliasing is used to try to combat this problem.

Anti aliasing

Anti aliasing is a process used to reduce the pixellated effect on images by smoothing the jagged appearance of diagonal lines in a bitmapped image.

Grids and fonts

Grids can be used as a basis for creating typography, with the letterforms built around the structure of a grid rather than being penned by hand or based on carved letterforms like traditional typographic forms.

ABCDEFGHIJKLMNOPQRSTUVWXYZ
abcdefghijklmnopqrstuvwxyz 1234567890

Foundry Gridnik Light

Often described as the thinking man's Courier, Foundry Gridnik is based on a font by Dutch designer Wim Crouwel, and takes its name from his devotion to the grid – he was often called 'Mr Gridnik' by his contemporaries in the 1960s.

ABCDEFGHIJKLMNOPQRSTUVWXYZ
abcdefghijklmnopqrstuvwxyz
1234567890

OCR–B

The OCR–B font was designed as an optical character recognition font (OCR) and as such can be scanned and turned back into editable text. To aid this process the characters are made additionally explicit to avoid any confusion, which would lead to scrambled text. The capital 'I' for example has exaggerated slab serifs so that it cannot be confused with the number '1'. The capital 'O' is very round in comparison to the number '0', again to prevent confusion. This is a monospaced font which means that all characters, however thin, occupy the same amount of space.

ABCDEFGHIJKLMNOPQRSTUVWXYZ
abcdefghijklmnopqrstuvwxyz1234567890

Dat Seventy

Dat Seventy is reminiscent of LED calculator display screens from the 1970s. The characters appear very square and have a space-age feel.

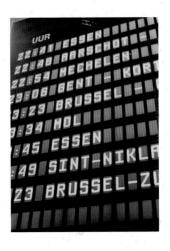

Above

The cover of *Vergezichten*, a book created by Dutch design studio Faydherbe / De Vringer, features text set on a visible grid of dots.

Above

This catalogue cover by Studio Myerscough features a simultaneously fluid and grid-based typeface. The simplicity of the typesetting complements the detail of the typeface.

Above

Environmental information signage has a distinct set of governing criteria. Legibility from a distance, absolute clarity of information and changeability, in the sense that the information often isn't static.

Above

These exhibition graphics were created by Studio Myerscough design studio with the text drawn on a strong grid that also appears on the accompanying literature and in the internal environmental space.

ABCDEFGHIJKLMNOPQRSTUVWXYZ
abcdefghijklmnopqrstuvwxyz 1234567890

Above

The font above was created by Swiss typographer Cornel Windlin in 1991 for issue 3 of font magazine *FUSE*, which focused on disinformation. Windlin used type generation software for the first time in the design, which was based on a pixelated printout of 4pt Akzidenz Grotesk that he cleaned up, restructured and partly redesigned.

Left

Posters for the Stedelijk Museum in Amsterdam by Cornel Windlin.

Generating type

While there are thousands of typefaces available, it is sometimes necessary to generate new ones. Fonts can be produced in a number of different ways from creating original art, replicating type from older publications, mark making or rendering type in font generation programs. The ability to create fonts electronically has opened the possibility to generate fonts quickly, in response to the specific needs and desires of clients, designers and typographers.

FF Stealth, above
FF Stealth has strong graphic presence. Created by Malcolm Garrett in 1995, it features minimalist forms reminiscent of occult symbols.

Atomic Circle, above
Atomic Circle created by Sylke Janetzky needs a certain amount of deciphering to understand how the small circles represent what the letters are.

Above
These are pages taken from the Diesel book produced by Spanish design studio Vasava Artworks. The book features typography of a highly graphic nature, such that the characters are on the verge of being lost in the image of which they form part. This can be seen clearly in the '5' and '1' which are heavily camouflaged by plant motifs. The words in the Diesel's Revolutions design (far left) are also subsumed by the image of which they are part.

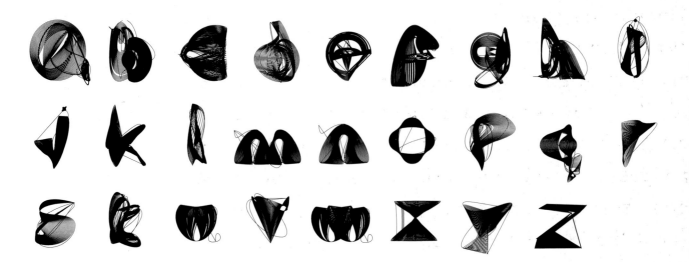

Above

This typeface was created by London design studio Research Studios to promote 'Made in Clerkenwell', an open event held in central London. To reflect the precise and crafted artisanal nature of the works exhibited (including ceramics, textiles and jewellery), a hand-drawn type was developed. The typeface was generated using vector paths, as these can be quickly manipulated to obtain the desired shape and style for each letter. Each character is created using lines of the same width, ensuring consistency and a degree of uniformity from letter to letter.

Below

This is a design created by Studio Myerscough design studio for webwizards, which uses a typeface inspired by the Slinky toy. The letters replicate the movements of a Slinky's coils.

Left

Pictured left are posters from font magazine *FUSE*. Far left is a Blockland & Rossum poster featuring a collage of made and found typographical elements. In the middle is Malcolm Garret's Stealth font poster, showing his experimental typeface *in situ*. Immediately left is Brett Wickens' typeface Crux95, with its distorted and manipulated forms.

Legibility and readability

These two terms are often used synonymously. Strictly speaking, *legibility* refers to the ability to distinguish one letterform from another through the physical characteristics inherent in a particular typeface, such as x-height, character shapes, counter size, stroke contrast and type weight. *Readability* concerns the properties of a piece of type or design that affect the ability to make it understood.

Ab

The decorative nature of the Benguiat font means that when set as body copy it can be hard to read, as the decorative elements impede the eye tracking across the text and break the reading flow. While characters at display size are clear, at smaller sizes legibility is compromised.

Ab

In contrast to the example above, Ionic is designed specifically for newspaper applications; its exaggerated serifs, large open counters and relatively large x-height means, it is easy to read over extended texts.

Whether something is readable or not has a dimension that goes beyond what the letters and words say. Something can be readable, inasmuch as you can take understanding from it, without necessarily being able to read it. Graffiti that is illegible allows people to read anger on the part of the protagonist, for example.

The fonts above (from top to bottom: Crash, Caustic Biomorph Extra Bold and Barnbrook Gothic Three) may not be the most legible, but under the right contexts they can inform the reader through their readability – character forms themselves convey an instant message in addition to the words they spell.

Below

Pictured below is the American Broadcasting Company (ABC) logo. It was designed by Paul Rand to be clear and instantly recognisable. This means that the logo can still be identified, even with a relatively poor quality reproduction.

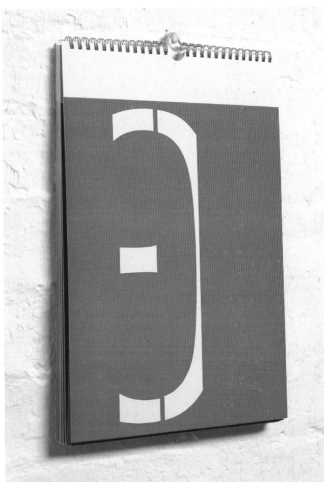

Left

This is a calendar created by design studio Struktur Design. It questions the very notion of legibility and readability. Each person is left to make up their own opinion as to what it says, with the normal clues that we look for reduced to a minimum.

Above

The Tate Galleries logos by Wolff Olins feature a non-static approach that conveys a sense of movement and fluidity, even though at first glance there appears to be reduced legibility. However, this increases the readability, or what we understand from the logotype.

Left

Sometimes the boundary between legibility and readability is a fine one, as the examples on this spread show. Pictured is an image by Scott Clum that appeared in issue 13 of font magazine *FUSE*, which focused on superstition. While the Burn typeface approximates the idea of streaks of flame well, it is far from the easiest to read.

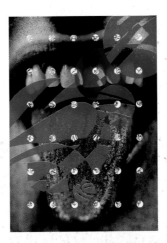

Left

This is a poster from issue 9 of font magazine *FUSE*, which features the typeface Auto by Vaughan Oliver. Each character is reversed out of a white circle, but their elaborate nature means they lack legibility as it is difficult to identify them at first glance from their physical characteristics.

Texture

Typography is just one element of a design, used in combination with images, diagrams, photography and other graphic elements. Type forms part of a larger visual and informative scheme. The vast array of typefaces available means that type can be used to add a great deal of texture to a design, as the examples in this spread show.

ABCDEFGHIJKLMNOPQRSTUVWXYZ

ABCDEFGHIJKLMNOPQRSTUVWXYZ

ABCDEFGHIJKLMNOPQRSTUVWXYZ

The fonts above (From top to bottom: Stamp Gothic, Attic and Confidential) show how texture can be added to a design. The fonts offer a facsimile of the patchy nature of other printing methods.

Above

These flyers were created by design studio Studio Output for Switch, a Friday night event at London nightclub Ministry of Sound. The thin, bendy type is styled like electrical wire in the three colours used for electrical appliances in the UK. Added texture and a homely feel are given to the flyers through the flock wallpaper design behind the light switches.

Above

These flyers were created by Studio Output design studio for a Section 8 Theatre event at the Ministry of Sound. The rich imagery created by the surreal photomontages evocative of cabaret is enhanced by the logotype that is styled like a woodcut.

Left and below

These spreads were created by design studio Vast Agency for *Shufti*, an experimental magazine. The blue type on the different pages overprints to create a soft, textured combination with the image and other type. The photo-rich magazine is printed on Reeves Design Bright White, which has a luxurious thick woven texture that adds a physical textural quality.

Above

Peter and Paul design studio add texture to these designs by overprinting type on the base image and subtly layering information.

Type as image

In addition to its function of using letters to communicate words, type is also used as a graphic device that speaks more through its visual representation than the meanings of the constituent letters. Logos are a common example of this as the styling of the letters is used to create a visual statement about a company or organisation.

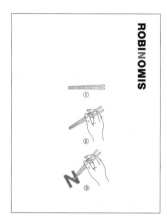

Above

Pictured is part of an identity created for legal firm Robin Simon LLP by Webb & Webb design studio. The 'N' that forms the last letter of the partners' names is used as a central element, picked out in colour throughout the identity. This 'N' is given life through various typographic exercises. For example, it becomes a noodle in the chopsticks.

Above

The CNN logo is a special ligature that conveys a visual clue to the activities of the company, a broadcast news channel.

Above

The IBM logo was designed by Paul Rand. The logo's horizontal lines make reference to binary information, the raw material of computing.

Above

The 'I Love New York' logo by Milton Glaser features a rebus of an eye-catching heart symbol as a visual substitution for the word 'love'.

Above

This logo by Thomas Manss & Co. for Metamorphosis hints at the transformation of a caterpillar to a butterfly, as represented by the chrysalis attached to the 'M'.

This page

All the handwritten type in this brochure was created by Webb & Webb design studio for an exhibition of chairs by Nicholas Von der Borch and Jeff Fisher. The result is a mix of words, drawn symbols, sketches and mis-spellings (such as 'suksesful disine'), which creates a strong, image-based visual impression. It also tips its hat to a surrealist painting by René Magritte *Ceci n'est pas une pipe* (This is not a pipe).

SUKSESFUL DISINE

TEST RESULTS	10/10		ORAL EXAM	
RIGOROUS	PITILESS	DRASTIC	7	10
STRINGENT	UNCOMPROMISING			
MERCILESS	NO QUARTER GIVEN		WIT	INTEGRITY
50			4·7	10
40			MATH	IRONY
30			5	10
20				
10				
WIND TUNNEL			SAFETY	ART
①	②	③	④	⑤
BEFORE	AFTER	TRUTH	BEAUTY	PATHOS

THIS IS NOT A CHAIR

Oak from the Von der Borch estate forest Westfalia GR
Some thanks to Antoine

SAFETY INSTRUCTIONS

1. Most of the component must fit into the board in correct direction. In some of these cases the components are marked accordingly. The hinges are neither marked by means of coloured rings nor direct labelling. In case of many small miniature components it is difficult to recognise the colour code or labelling. We therefore recomend to check value of resistor before filling.

2. Usually a holder for the IC is attached. If necessary the connecting pins have to be bent a bit (with a small pair of pliers) For this purpose a narrow side of the case is marked; with a notch, a point impression, a deepened triangle or something like that. In rare cases the vertical is not marked at all.

3. These products do not have any CE acceptance. May contain substances which are harmful to the body. Dangerous situations may occur during starting when making a mistake (e.g. cables may glow or catch fire) The presence of a competant person is always necessary during mounting. If the module or device does not work properly, accidents happened (liquid ran into the device, device fell down etc.) or if it causes strange noises or smells, switch off immediately. Ask an expert for examination.

4. BORCH/FISHER disclaim any responsibility for anything they have done in the past or anything they might do in the future.

2½ dimensions. We are chair 𝄂𝄂𝄂 Why the bottom is so important Comfort leads to idleness. GOOD POSTURE leads 𝄂𝄂 to glory. Comfort ⊙▼⊙ is an illusion. You never relax in a good chair. (B)(F) devote their lives to this. → Start from a drawing of a chair, extrapolate into a 3D object. The result is a sculpture of a drawing. (B)(F) look at the chair from 2½ directions, & impossibly, have reinvented the chair. The middle ground between 2D & 3D is a landscape (B)(F) will ultimately widen to encompass everything. Nicholas Von der Borch & Jeff Fisher are chair.

Concrete poetry, typograms, trompe l'œil and calligrammes

Text presentation can be used as a key component of a design job. It is possible to create a visual element from the placement of the words themselves, as the examples on this spread illustrate.

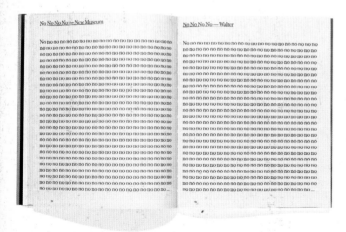

Above

This book was created by Cartlidge Levene design studio for an exhibition of the work of sound installation artist Bruce Nauman at London's Tate Modern Gallery. The book features spreads that are set with type patterns referring to his works, in an attempt to visually convey with static text the playfulness of the sounds in his works and their aural repetition.

Concrete poetry

Concrete poetry is experimental poetry from the 1950-1960s that concentrated on the visual appearance of words through the use of different typographical arrangements, such as the use of shaped text blocks and collage. The intent of the poet is conveyed by the shape the poem takes rather than a conventional reading of the words. As concrete poetry is visual, its effect is lost when a poem is read aloud.

Typograms

A typogram refers to the deliberate use of typography to express an idea visually, but by incorporating something more than just the letters that constitute the word. For example, the word 'half' cut in half and displayed with only half visible letters would be a typogram.

Trompe l'œil

Meaning 'trick of the eye' a *trompe l'œil* is an optical illusion in which a design is made to look like something it is not, as can be seen in the book design on the opposite page (bottom left).

Calligramme

French writer Guillaume Apollinaire invented calligrammes in 1918, which he described as 'painting with words'. From the Greek, *callos*, meaning 'beauty', and *gram/graph*, meaning 'written' or 'write', a calligramme is a word, phrase or poem that is written so that it forms an image of the subject of the text. A famous calligramme is *Il pleut*, where the letters rain down the page driving vertically.

Right

Pictured right is the cover and inside of an invitation created by Webb & Webb design studio for an event at Hogarth's House in London. To convey a sense of the festivities, the name of the institution is split or wrapped around from the cover to the inner to produce the jolly 'Ho Ho' typogram.

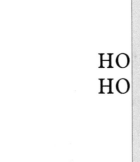

Right

This poster was created by Angus Hyland at Pentagram design studio for the London College of Printing to promote an exhibition of logos created by the design studio. The word 'Symbol' has been turned into a logotype to illustrate the nature of what logotypes can become.

Right

The text in this design by Spanish design studio Vasava Artworks is in the vein of concrete poetry, in that it forms the leaves attached to the stem of the apple.

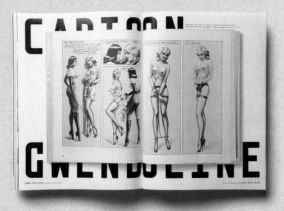

Above

Pictured above are spreads from *Zembla* magazine created by design studio Frost Design. The spreads feature *trompe l'œils* devices that give the impression of articles and other publications overlaying the pages of the publication itself. However, these are actually part of the design.

Type in the environment

Typography surrounds us, and its application is not always what we would expect. Type is present in the environment in many ways, from the wording on posters to signage and artistic installations. Type in the environment tends to be large scale so that it can be seen at a greater distance, and it is perhaps the scale that makes it so intriguing.

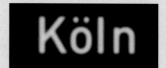

It may sound obvious, but perfect consistency can be crucial in signage projects. The signage system used on the roads in the UK was created by Margaret Calvert, beginning in 1958. This system features lettering drawn with a large x-height that brings uniform clarity, with type reinforced by shape and colour. Blue and circles are orders or instructions; red and

triangles serve as a warnings; boxes or rectangles give information; and the hexagonal 'Stop' sign almost serves as a physical barrier. Although not universal, this system has been replicated to a greater or lesser extent in many other countries, albeit with different typography.

The DIN-Schrift typeface is used on German road signage. As this is often reversed out of black and viewed in poor conditions, the letterforms have been tweaked to add clarity. For example, the counter of the 'o' has been made more oval, letters have been lengthened, and the umlaut diacritical mark has been made circular rather than square.

The images above show the original typeface and how it can be seen in poor visibility (left) and the enhanced typeface and how it can be seen in poor visibility (right).

Above

This signage at the Euston showroom of Steelcase Strafor in London was created by Studio Myerscough design studio. The letterforms have been fabricated from sheet steel to give a solid, three-dimensional feel.

Below

Type can occupy unexpected places in the environment, as this exhibition for Archigram created by Studio Myerscough design studio shows, with deckchair canvas used as the substrate.

Left

This kiosk installation was created by design studio Vasava Artworks for the Institut Català del Sòl - Generalitat de Catalunya for the Barcelona Meeting Point property fair. The display features larger than life characters for the number '42,000', the number of apartments to be built as part of a construction project.

Scale

Type can be produced in a range of different sizes, which means its use is not limited to the pages of a publication, where a point or two can make all the difference. Type can be larger than life, adopting a physical presence in the environment, as the examples on this spread show.

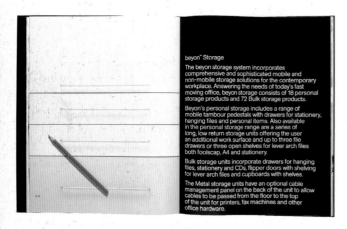

Above

This design by Studio Myerscough design studio and Allford Hall Monaghan Morris architects uses type at a large scale to indicate specific areas for children's activities such as netball, football and basketball, where it is intended to be fun, engaging and ultimately informative.

Above

This signage at London Barbican was created by design studios Studio Myerscough and Cartlidge Levene. The large-scale signage wraps around the building like a second skin, with apertures cut away that allow the building to show through.

Above

The Beyon furniture brochure by design studio SEA Design features photographs capturing close-up details, such as the joints in the furniture, that are supported with large type. In this way, the type reinforces the perception of quality furniture production that the images present.

Right

This cover was created by design studio Frost Design and features a single letterpressed ampersand character at a monumental scale to represent the Ampersan& logotype.

Far right

This signage at London's Tea Building was created by Studio Myerscough design studio and features the simple beauty of a bespoke font that serves as signage and a focal point. The rawness of the application is apt for the building that contains many textures and exposed materials.

Above

This environment was created by Studio Myerscough design studio. The typography plays a central role in the learning environment to help inform, inspire and guide.

Above

This installation was created by designer Gavin Ambrose for the British Design Council to reduce complex statistical information to single 'facts' that invite the viewer to interact with them. The explanation or significance of each number is screen printed on the side of its constructed form and viewers are actively encouraged to sit on and explore the letterforms. The font used is a heavy version of Helvetica, the Design Council's corporate font.

Below

Pictured is the Vietnam War Memorial in Washington, USA. The scale of the monument and the number of names results in an imposing structure that conveys a sense of gravity and meaning. The wall confronts the viewer with simple, subtle, understated lettering; it is also powerfully aggressive as the names run on endlessly. The typography helps to convey a sense of contemplative reflection.

Vernacular

Vernacular is the everyday language spoken by a group of people that includes slang and regional phrasing. It is the language of the street, no matter where that street is. To a certain extent, the textures of vernacular can be communicated in text through the use of typography. Type has personality and from the typographic choices made, text can be instilled with the personality of the typeface, whether conservative, authoritarian, young or rebellious.

Many fonts have a heritage that can be traced back to physical objects in the environment featuring text, some of which are shown below.

The Tape Type font utilises the random patterns and irregular lines of packaging tape to create a clumsy and textured effect.

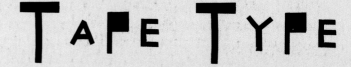

Inspired by electronic display systems, the LED font is based on a simplified grid of seven bars.

Stencil, created by Gerry Powell in 1938, looks industrial and durable, possibly mass produced or shipped from afar.

Crud font looks like a typewriter font that has been used extensively and has badly deteriorated.

These images created for various projects by Studio Myerscough design studio demonstrate the power of vernacular typography. In these examples, the typography reinforces the literal meanings of the words they present. This association affects the whole design, whether the bright show lights and glamour for the Rock Style exhibition or the expressive raw quality of the type used on retail items manufactured by the studio.

Appropriation

Appropriation is the borrowing of aesthetic elements from a particular epoch, style or movement and using them as part of another. Appropriated elements frequently have denotive and/or cognitive meanings that continue to function in their new role; this sometimes places them in a different historical context and subverts them.

The new context can be so overwhelming that the original source of the appropriation is forgotten. Perhaps the most infamous example of this is the swastika. For 3,000 years it was a symbol of good luck and prosperity for societies including Hindus, Buddhists, Greeks, Romans, Aztecs, Persians and ancient Jewish peoples. Appropriated by Nazi Germany it became a symbol of power and fear, representing the struggle for the victory of the Aryan man.

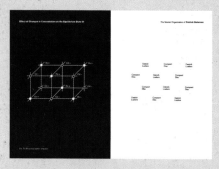
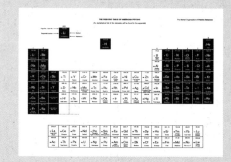

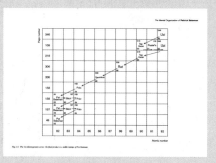

The periodic table of the elements adorns the walls of classrooms around the world. Appropriated by Gavin Ambrose and Matt Lumby, key words from *American Psycho*, a novel by Bret Easton Ellis, are allocated positions in the periodic table. 'Ag' passes from being the symbol for 'silver' to become the symbol for 'agony', for example. Chemical formulae such as that for the classification of matter (top left) create poems from the word groupings.

Pictured below is a signage system created for a retail store by designer Gavin Ambrose. The industrial lettering was influenced by stencilled street graphics such as the anti-Nazi slogan sprayed on a wall in Germany, above.

Commercial projects often draw inspiration from real events and historic designs. Pictured right is an example from design studio Vasava Artworks, inspired by Communist propaganda posters such as the one above from Vietnam. The Vasava Artworks design was created for a fashion spread called Friostroika in the EP3 section of Spanish newspaper *El País*.

Typographic democracy

Traditionally typography was a time-consuming specialist pursuit, generally undertaken at type foundries.

Technological developments such as personal computers and the software packages that operate on them have democratised font development, reducing the barriers – particularly time – that previously restricted development to a handful of professional typographers. A designer can now produce type quickly for a specific job within or outside of traditional typographical confines, while he or she juggles other pieces of work. In the same liberating vein as Letraset, technological development means that type no longer has to be formal or developed by dedicated typographers.

Above

Anarchic qualities are translated to exhibition graphics in this installation by Studio Myerscough for Archigram. The freedom of the typography is both engaging and informative.

Above

This is an image created by Webb & Webb design studio for a corporate publication about exhibition and events company Touchstone. The hand image conveys attributes the company feels it possesses such as 'professional' and 'innovative'. The fact that the letters are hand-rendered softens and gives a human touch to comments such as 'unique' that, if set formally, would appear immodest.

Above

This image by Studio KA design studio features text in blocky yellow capitals that perhaps mimic how someone might write bold capitals on a piece of paper.

Above

This is a poster created for an architecture exhibition by Chilean design studio Y&R. It features a capital 'A' drawn like a solid structure, representing architecture. The crossbar in the form of an eye refers to the fact that at an exhibition a visitor looks at things.

Ownership

Designs and typography can be so successful that they become inextricably linked to the products, organisations or events that they were created for.

Times New Roman was designed for *The Times* newspaper and focused on expressing authoritative legibility.

Apple Macintosh uses a condensed Garamond in its marketing material, which strengthens Apple's relatively abstract logo to give logical consistency.

The Adidas brand is recognisable from the dynamic, geometric letterforms of Herb Lubalin's Avant Garde.

Confectionery brand M&M uses the distinctive slab serif Rockwell, which gives it a fun feel.

The titling on the Beach Boys 1966 album *Pet Sounds* used Copper Black, forever linking it to the 1960s, though the typeface was actually created in 1921.

Futura, based on simple functional forms, has been used by German auto manufacturer Volkswagen since the 1960s.

FASHION MAGAZINE *VOGUE* USES THE DISTINCTIVE AND ELEGANT BODONI LETTERFORMS THAT HAVE FINE SERIFS.

Absolut Vodka uses a condensed, extra bold version of Futura that results in an interesting contrast between x-height and ascender length.

Internet shopping website **amazon**.com uses Officina Sans in both bold and book for a no-nonsense look.

The London Underground uses Johnston's masterpiece sans serif typeface that bears his name.

London Underground was later revisited and amended by Eric Gill, the revised form of which is used by clothing label Benetton, among others.

The identity of branding and communications agency Osmosis has no definable logo. Instead, it features a series of 'O's in different typefaces that change with each application. This is part of a strategy to develop ownership of the letter over a period of time, as it becomes an intrinsic part of Osmosis' visual identity. Three-dimensional 'O's were created in a range of colours to be photographed in different environments and used on business cards and literature.

proof marks

Proofreading marks are a set of correctional marks that allow printers, designers, editors and their clients to communicate text changes accurately and without misinterpretation. Text can be marked up or proofed by a client and returned to the designer for the changes to be made. For example, the <> symbols are used to denote increase and decrease. This can be used with type size or leading. The correctional marks are written on to a proof, both in the text itself and in the margin, so that it can be clearly seen where a correction is to be made. Although falling out of usage with general clients, they are still prevalent in book and magazine publishing.

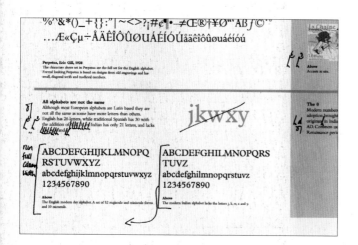

Text in the process of being proofed. The proof marks can be seen in the text as well as in the margin space. An understanding of the use of these marks is essential to be able to correct a print job efficiently, accurately, and most importantly, without introducing additional errors.

~~Strike through is used to indicate text that will be replaced later.~~

~~When the final text is inserted the strike though can be removed.~~

~~Deletions in legal documents are also made using strike through~~

~~so that people can see what has been, or is to be, removed.~~

Instruction	Text mark	Margin Mark	Instruction	Text mark	Margin Mark
Leave as printed	Crack/back	STET	Indent one em	Typeface	□/
Delete	Typeface/	ℐ	Vertical align	Typeface	\\\\
Delete and close up gap	Type/face	ℐ	Raise or lower	Typeface	⊤
Delete and leave space	Crack/back	#	Abbreviation or numeral to be spelt out	10 point Nine pt	Spell out
New matter to be inserted	⋏ size	Type ⋏	Substitute for individual letters	Trompe l'œil	o e /
Change to lowercase	TYPEface	l.c.	Use ligature or dipthong	Trompe l'œil	œ
Change to capital letters	typeface	Caps	New paragraph	of serifs. There are many types	N.P.
Change to small capitals	TYPEFACE	s.c.	No new paragraph	of serifs. There are many	RUN ON
Change to italics	Typeface	itals	Insert punctuation as indicated	Typeface⋏	⁏
Change to Roman	Typeface	ROM	Substitute punctuation mark indicated	Typeface/	⊙/
Change to bold	Typeface	bold	Insert em or en rule as indicated	Body/copy	⁗⋏
Wrong font used, replace	Typeface	w.f.	Insert parentheses or square-brackets	⋏Typeface⋏	c/⊐
Close up space	Typeface	⌢	Insert single quotes or double-quotes as indicated	⋏Typeface⋏	⸲ ⸳
Insert space	Font/usage	#⋏	Refer	Founts	⟨?⟩
Reduce space	Font /usage	# less	Substitute inferior	Typeface	⸲
Adjust leading	Font usage	<2pts #	Substitute superior	Typeface	⸰
Transpose	font check usage	+ RS	Underline	Typeface	insert rule
Move to right/indent	Font usage	⊏			
Take matter over to next line	Text needs to be returned.	T.O.			
Insert hyphen	type/face	/—/			

conclusion

Typography is an essential communication and design element that has evolved over several centuries, and continues to evolve as tastes continually change and technological development makes it easier to develop new typefaces.

Type plays a fundamental role in the communication process as much through the shapes and styling of the letterforms as the actual words that they form.

This volume has attempted to outline the origins of type and show how it has developed through time to provide a base of information that can be used to inform typographical decision making. This volume has also attempted to show how type can be used creatively to enhance communication and produce visual impact, in addition to identifying key norms to guide type usage.

Typography can be a complex subject filled with technical terms and jargon, which have been defined and explained to facilitate more precise communication of requirements.

We would like to thank everyone who has been involved in the production of this volume, especially all the designers and design studios that generously contributed examples of their work. And a final big thank you to Natalia Price-Cabrera, Brian Morris and Lorna Fray at AVA Publishing for all their help and support.

contacts

glossary

Apex
The point formed at the top of a character such as 'A' where the left and right strokes meet.

Arm
See *Bar*.

Ascender
See *Descender*.

Bar
The horizontal stroke on characters 'A', 'H', 'T', 'e', 'f', 't'. Sometimes called a *crossbar* on 'A' and 'H' or arm on 'F', 'T', 'E' and 'K' upstroke.

Baseline
The baseline is an imaginary line upon which a line of text sits and is the point from which other elements of type are measured including *x-height* and *leading*.

Black letter
A typeface based on the ornate writing prevalent during the Middle Ages. Also called block, gothic, old English, black or broken.

Body text
Body text or copy is the text that forms the main part of a work. It is usually between 8 and 14 *points* in size.

Bold
A version of the *Roman* with a wider *stroke*. Also called medium, semibold, black, super or poster.

Boldface type
A thick, heavy variety of type used to give emphasis.

Bowl
The *stroke* that surrounds and contains the *counter*.

Bracket
The curved portion of a *serif* that connects it to the *stroke*.

Character
An individual element of type such as a letter or punctuation mark.

Chin
The *terminal* angled part of the 'G'.

Condensed
A narrower version of the *Roman* cut.

Counter
The empty space inside the body stroke surrounded by the bowl.

Cross stroke
Horizontal stroke that crosses over the *stem*.

Crossbar
See *Bar*.

Crotch
Where the *leg* and *arm* of the 'K' and 'k' meet.

Cursive
Inclined *typeface* exhibiting calligraphic qualities. Used to describe true *italics*, as opposed to slanted *obliques* of *Roman* forms.

Deboss
As *emboss* but recessed into the *substrate*.

Descender
The part of a letter that falls below the baseline (descender).

Die cut
Special shapes cut into a *substrate* by a steel rule.

Display type
Large and/or distinctive type intended to attract the eye. Specifically cut to be viewed from a distance.

Dot gain
Dot gain describes the enlarging of ink dots on the printing stock and is something that occurs naturally as the ink is absorbed into the stock.

Down stroke
The heavy *stroke* in a type character.

Drop capital
A capital letter set in a larger *point* size and aligned with the top of the first line.

Ear
Decorative flourish on the upper right side of the 'g' *bowl*.

Em
Unit of measurement derived from the width of the square body of the cast upper case 'M'. An em equals the size of a given type, i.e. the em of 10 *point* type is 10 points.

Emboss
A design stamped without ink or foil giving a raised surface.

En
Unit of measurement equal to half of one *em*.

Extended
A wider version of the *Roman* cut.

Eye
A *counter*, specifically of 'e'.

Font
The physical attributes needed to make a typeface be it film, metal, wood or *PostScript* information.

Foot
Serif at the bottom of the *stem* that sits on the *baseline*.

Geometric
Sans serif fonts that are based on geometric shapes identifiable by round 'O' and 'Q' letters.

Golden section / golden ratio
A division in the ratio 8:13 that produces harmonious proportions.

Gothic
A *typeface* without *serifs*. Also called sans serif or lineale.

Gravure
A high volume *intaglio* printing process in which the printing area is etched into the printing plate.

Hairline
The thinnest *stroke* in a *typeface* that has varying widths. Also refers to a 0.25pt line, the thinnest line that can be confidently produced by printing processes.

Hand drawn
Typography that is hand made.

Hierarchy
A logical, organised and visual guide for text headings that indicates different levels of importance.

Hook
Serif at the top of a *stem*.

Ink trapping
The adjustment of areas of colour, text or shapes to account for misregistration on the printing press by overlapping them.

Intaglio
A technique that describes the printing of an image from a recessed design that is incised or etched into the surface of a plate. The ink lies recessed below the surface of the plate and transfers to the stock under pressure and stands in relief on the stock.

Italic
A version of the *Roman* cut that angles to the right at 7-20 degrees.

Kerning
The removal of unwanted space between letters.

Kerning pairs
Letter combinations that frequently need to be kerned.

Knockout
Where an underlaying colour has a gap inserted where another colour would overprint it. The bottom colour is knocked out to prevent colour mixing.

Leading
The space between lines of type measured from *baseline* to baseline. It is expressed in *points* and is a term derived from hot metal type printing when strips of lead were placed between lines of type to provide line spacing.

Leg
The lower, down sloping stroke of the 'K', 'k' and 'R'. Sometimes used for the *tail* of a 'Q'.

Legibility
The ability to distinguish one letter from another due to characteristics inherent in the *typeface* design.

Ligatures
The joining of two or three separate characters to form a single unit to avoid interference between certain letter combinations.

Light
A version of the *Roman* cut with a lighter *stroke*.

Lining numerals
Lining figures are numerals that share the same height and rest on the *baseline*.

Link
The part that joins the two *counters* of the double-storey 'g'.

Loop
The enclosed or partially enclosed lower *counter* in a *Roman* e.g. double-storey 'g'. Sometimes used to describe the *cursive* 'p' and 'b'.

Lowercase
See *Minuscules*.

Majuscules
Capital letters. Also called uppercase.

Meanline
Imaginary line that runs across the tops of non-ascending characters.

Measure
The length of a line of text expressed in *picas*.

Minuscule
Characters originated from the Carolingian letters. Also called *lowercase*.

Monospaced
Where each character occupies a space with the same width.

Oblique
A slanted version of *Roman* whose letterforms are essentially those of the Roman form. Mistakenly called *italics*.

Old Style
Old Style, Antiqua, Ancient, Renaissance, Baroque, Venetian or Garalde is a typeface style developed by Renaissance typographers that was based on Roman inscriptions. It was created to replace the black letter type and is characterised by low stroke contrast, bracketed *serifs*, and a left inclining stress.

Old Style figures
Numerals that vary in height and do not sit on the same baseline.

Overprint
Where one printing ink is printed over another.

Pica
A measurement for specifying line lengths. One pica is 12 *points* (UK/US) or 4.22mm. There are six picas to an inch.

Point system
The measurement for specifying typographical dimensions. The British and American point is 1/72 of an inch. The European Didot system provides similar size values.

PostScript
A page description language used by laser printers and on-screen graphics systems.

Quad
A non-printing metal block used a as a spacing device.

Readability
The overall visual representation of the text narrative.

Rebus
A visual puzzle where the participant has to decode a message that consists of pictures, which have been used to represent syllables and words.

Registration
The alignment of printing plates to create a cohesive image or reproduction.

Roman
The basic letterform.

Sans serif
A font without decorative serifs. Typically with little stroke thickness variation, a larger x-height and no stress in rounded strokes.

Script
A *typeface* designed to imitate handwriting.

Serif
A small *stroke* at the end of a main vertical or horizontal stroke. Also used as a classification for typefaces that contain such decorative rounded, pointed, square, or *slab serif* finishing strokes.

Shoulder or body
The arch formed on the 'h'.

Slab serif
A fonts with heavy, squared off finishing *strokes*, low contrast and few curves.

Small caps
Small caps are *majuscules* that are close in size to the *minuscules* of a given *typeface*. They are less domineering than regular size capitals and are used setting acronyms and common abbreviations.

Spine
The left to right curving *stroke* in 'S' and 's'.

Spur
The end of the curved part of 'C' or 'S'.

Stem
The main vertical or diagonal *stroke* of a letter.

Stress
The direction in which a curved *stroke* changes weight.

Stroke
The diagonal portion of letterforms such as 'N', 'M', or 'Y'. *Stems*, *bars*, *arms*, *bowls* etc are collectively referred to as *strokes*.

Substrate
Any surface or material that is to be printed upon.

Surprint
See *Overprint*.

Tail
Descending *stroke* on 'Q', 'K' or 'R'. *Descenders* on 'g', 'j', 'p', 'q', and 'y' may also be called tails.

Terminal
A curve such as a *tail*, *link*, *ear* or *loop*, also called finial. A ball terminal combines a tail dot or circular stroke with a hook at the end of a *tail* or *arm*. A beak terminal is a sharp *spur* at the end of an arm.

Text
Written or printed matter that forms the body of a publication.

Tracking
The adjustable amount of space between letters.

Typeface
The letters, numbers and punctuation marks of a type design.

Typeface family
A series of *typefaces* sharing common characteristics but with different sizes and weights.

Type styles
The different visual appearances of typefaces.

Uppercase
See *Majuscules*.

Upstroke
The finer stroke of a type character.

Vertex
The angle formed at the bottom where the left and right *strokes* meet, such as with the 'V'.

X-height
The height of the lowercase 'x' of a given typeface.

index

font index